C++.NET AND OLEDB

OLEDB

Working with the Dataview

Richard Thomas Edwards

CONTENTS

WHY IS THE CODE BROKEN INTO SECTIONS?

This book is really condensed

THIS BOOK IS REALL A HUGE BOOK! It just doesn't look that way if you're looking at just the length of it. For example, if you were to eliminate the stylesheets, there are approximately 68 pages before I added one – just one – example of a complete code example. In-other-words, 6 pages of one code example is almost 10 percent of this book. Imagine what 5760 would look like at just 5 pages each! This book would wind up being 28800 pages in length.

Yet, it is, indeed, all here!

```
System::String^ cnstr  = "";
System::String^ strQuery = "";

System::Data::OleDb::OleDbConnection^ cn = gcnew
System::Data::OleDb::OleDbConnection();
cn->ConnectionString = cnstr;
cn->Open();

System::Data::OleDb::OleDbCommand^ cmd = gcnew
System::Data::OleDb::OleDbCommand();
Cmd->Connection = cn;
Cmd->CommandType = System::Data::CommandType::Text;
Cmd->CommandText = strQuery;
```

```
Cmd->ExecuteNonquery();

System::Data::OleDb::OleDbDataAdapter^ da = gcnew
System::Data::OleDb::OleDbDataAdapter(cmd);

System::Data::DataTable^ dt = gcnew System::Data::DataTable();
da->Fill(dt);
   System::Data::DataView^ dv = dt->DefaultView;
   Scripting::FileSystemObject^ fso = gcnew Scripting::FileSystemObject();
   Scripting::TextStream^ txtstream = fso->OpenTextFile(Application::StartupPath +
"\\Products.html",Scripting::IOMode::ForWriting, true,
Scripting::Tristate::TristateUseDefault);
   txtstream->WriteLine("<html>");
   txtstream->WriteLine("<head>");
   txtstream->WriteLine("<title>Products</title>");
   txtstream->WriteLine("<style type='text/css'>");
   txtstream->WriteLine("body");
   txtstream->WriteLine("{");
   txtstream->WriteLine("    PADDING-RIGHT: 0px;");
   txtstream->WriteLine("    PADDING-LEFT: 0px;");
   txtstream->WriteLine("    PADDING-BOTTOM: 0px;");
   txtstream->WriteLine("    MARGIN: 0px;");
   txtstream->WriteLine("    COLOR: #333;");
   txtstream->WriteLine("    PADDING-TOP: 0px;");
   txtstream->WriteLine("    FONT-FAMILY: verdana, arial, helvetica, sans-serif;");
   txtstream->WriteLine("}");
   txtstream->WriteLine("table");
   txtstream->WriteLine("{");
   txtstream->WriteLine("    BORDER-RIGHT: #999999 1px solid;");
   txtstream->WriteLine("    PADDING-RIGHT: 1px;");
   txtstream->WriteLine("    PADDING-LEFT: 1px;");
   txtstream->WriteLine("    PADDING-BOTTOM: 1px;");
   txtstream->WriteLine("    LINE-HEIGHT: 8px;");
   txtstream->WriteLine("    PADDING-TOP: 1px;");
   txtstream->WriteLine("    BORDER-BOTTOM: #999 1px solid;");
   txtstream->WriteLine("    BACKGROUND-COLOR: #eeeeee;");
   txtstream->WriteLine("    filter:progid:DXImageTransform->Microsoft-
>Shadow(color='silver', Direction=135, Strength=16)");
   txtstream->WriteLine("}");
   txtstream->WriteLine("th");
   txtstream->WriteLine("{");
   txtstream->WriteLine("    BORDER-RIGHT: #999999 3px solid;");
   txtstream->WriteLine("    PADDING-RIGHT: 6px;");
   txtstream->WriteLine("    PADDING-LEFT: 6px;");
   txtstream->WriteLine("    FONT-WEIGHT: Bold;");
   txtstream->WriteLine("    FONT-SIZE: 14px;");
   txtstream->WriteLine("    PADDING-BOTTOM: 6px;");
   txtstream->WriteLine("    COLOR: darkred;");
   txtstream->WriteLine("    LINE-HEIGHT: 14px;");
   txtstream->WriteLine("    PADDING-TOP: 6px;");
```

```
txtstream->WriteLine("    BORDER-BOTTOM: #999 1px solid;");
txtstream->WriteLine("    BACKGROUND-COLOR: #eeeeee;");
txtstream->WriteLine("    FONT-FAMILY: font-family: Cambria, serif;");
txtstream->WriteLine("    FONT-SIZE: 12px;");
txtstream->WriteLine("    text-align: left;");
txtstream->WriteLine("    white-Space: nowrap='nowrap';");
txtstream->WriteLine("}");
txtstream->WriteLine("->th");
txtstream->WriteLine("{");
txtstream->WriteLine("    BORDER-RIGHT: #999999 2px solid;");
txtstream->WriteLine("    PADDING-RIGHT: 6px;");
txtstream->WriteLine("    PADDING-LEFT: 6px;");
txtstream->WriteLine("    FONT-WEIGHT: Bold;");
txtstream->WriteLine("    PADDING-BOTTOM: 6px;");
txtstream->WriteLine("    COLOR: black;");
txtstream->WriteLine("    PADDING-TOP: 6px;");
txtstream->WriteLine("    BORDER-BOTTOM: #999 2px solid;");
txtstream->WriteLine("    BACKGROUND-COLOR: #eeeeee;");
txtstream->WriteLine("    FONT-FAMILY: font-family: Cambria, serif;");
txtstream->WriteLine("    FONT-SIZE: 10px;");
txtstream->WriteLine("    text-align: right;");
txtstream->WriteLine("    white-Space: nowrap='nowrap';");
txtstream->WriteLine("}");
txtstream->WriteLine("td");
txtstream->WriteLine("{");
txtstream->WriteLine("    BORDER-RIGHT: #999999 3px solid;");
txtstream->WriteLine("    PADDING-RIGHT: 6px;");
txtstream->WriteLine("    PADDING-LEFT: 6px;");
txtstream->WriteLine("    FONT-WEIGHT: Normal;");
txtstream->WriteLine("    PADDING-BOTTOM: 6px;");
txtstream->WriteLine("    COLOR: navy;");
txtstream->WriteLine("    LINE-HEIGHT: 14px;");
txtstream->WriteLine("    PADDING-TOP: 6px;");
txtstream->WriteLine("    BORDER-BOTTOM: #999 1px solid;");
txtstream->WriteLine("    BACKGROUND-COLOR: #eeeeee;");
txtstream->WriteLine("    FONT-FAMILY: font-family: Cambria, serif;");
txtstream->WriteLine("    FONT-SIZE: 12px;");
txtstream->WriteLine("    text-align: left;");
txtstream->WriteLine("    white-Space: nowrap='nowrap';");
txtstream->WriteLine("}");
txtstream->WriteLine("div");
txtstream->WriteLine("{");
txtstream->WriteLine("    BORDER-RIGHT: #999999 3px solid;");
txtstream->WriteLine("    PADDING-RIGHT: 6px;");
txtstream->WriteLine("    PADDING-LEFT: 6px;");
txtstream->WriteLine("    FONT-WEIGHT: Normal;");
txtstream->WriteLine("    PADDING-BOTTOM: 6px;");
txtstream->WriteLine("    COLOR: white;");
txtstream->WriteLine("    PADDING-TOP: 6px;");
txtstream->WriteLine("    BORDER-BOTTOM: #999 1px solid;");
```

```
txtstream->WriteLine("   BACKGROUND-COLOR: navy;");
txtstream->WriteLine("   FONT-FAMILY: font-family: Cambria, serif;");
txtstream->WriteLine("   FONT-SIZE: 10px;");
txtstream->WriteLine("   text-align: left;");
txtstream->WriteLine("   white-Space: nowrap='nowrap';");
txtstream->WriteLine("}");
txtstream->WriteLine("span");
txtstream->WriteLine("{");
txtstream->WriteLine("   BORDER-RIGHT: #999999 3px solid;");
txtstream->WriteLine("   PADDING-RIGHT: 3px;");
txtstream->WriteLine("   PADDING-LEFT: 3px;");
txtstream->WriteLine("   FONT-WEIGHT: Normal;");
txtstream->WriteLine("   PADDING-BOTTOM: 3px;");
txtstream->WriteLine("   COLOR: white;");
txtstream->WriteLine("   PADDING-TOP: 3px;");
txtstream->WriteLine("   BORDER-BOTTOM: #999 1px solid;");
txtstream->WriteLine("   BACKGROUND-COLOR: navy;");
txtstream->WriteLine("   FONT-FAMILY: font-family: Cambria, serif;");
txtstream->WriteLine("   FONT-SIZE: 10px;");
txtstream->WriteLine("   text-align: left;");
txtstream->WriteLine("   white-Space: nowrap='nowrap';");
txtstream->WriteLine("   display: inline-block;");
txtstream->WriteLine("   width: 100%;");
txtstream->WriteLine("}");
txtstream->WriteLine("textarea");
txtstream->WriteLine("{");
txtstream->WriteLine("   BORDER-RIGHT: #999999 3px solid;");
txtstream->WriteLine("   PADDING-RIGHT: 3px;");
txtstream->WriteLine("   PADDING-LEFT: 3px;");
txtstream->WriteLine("   FONT-WEIGHT: Normal;");
txtstream->WriteLine("   PADDING-BOTTOM: 3px;");
txtstream->WriteLine("   COLOR: white;");
txtstream->WriteLine("   PADDING-TOP: 3px;");
txtstream->WriteLine("   BORDER-BOTTOM: #999 1px solid;");
txtstream->WriteLine("   BACKGROUND-COLOR: navy;");
txtstream->WriteLine("   FONT-FAMILY: font-family: Cambria, serif;");
txtstream->WriteLine("   FONT-SIZE: 10px;");
txtstream->WriteLine("   text-align: left;");
txtstream->WriteLine("   white-Space: nowrap='nowrap';");
txtstream->WriteLine("   width: 100%;");
txtstream->WriteLine("}");
txtstream->WriteLine("select");
txtstream->WriteLine("{");
txtstream->WriteLine("   BORDER-RIGHT: #999999 3px solid;");
txtstream->WriteLine("   PADDING-RIGHT: 6px;");
txtstream->WriteLine("   PADDING-LEFT: 6px;");
txtstream->WriteLine("   FONT-WEIGHT: Normal;");
txtstream->WriteLine("   PADDING-BOTTOM: 6px;");
txtstream->WriteLine("   COLOR: white;");
txtstream->WriteLine("   PADDING-TOP: 6px;");
```

```
txtstream->WriteLine("   BORDER-BOTTOM: #999 1px solid;");
txtstream->WriteLine("   BACKGROUND-COLOR: navy;");
txtstream->WriteLine("   FONT-FAMILY: font-family: Cambria, serif;");
txtstream->WriteLine("   FONT-SIZE: 10px;");
txtstream->WriteLine("   text-align: left;");
txtstream->WriteLine("   white-Space: nowrap='nowrap';");
txtstream->WriteLine("   width: 100%;");
txtstream->WriteLine("}");
txtstream->WriteLine("input");
txtstream->WriteLine("{");
txtstream->WriteLine("   BORDER-RIGHT: #999999 3px solid;");
txtstream->WriteLine("   PADDING-RIGHT: 3px;");
txtstream->WriteLine("   PADDING-LEFT: 3px;");
txtstream->WriteLine("   FONT-WEIGHT: Bold;");
txtstream->WriteLine("   PADDING-BOTTOM: 3px;");
txtstream->WriteLine("   COLOR: white;");
txtstream->WriteLine("   PADDING-TOP: 3px;");
txtstream->WriteLine("   BORDER-BOTTOM: #999 1px solid;");
txtstream->WriteLine("   BACKGROUND-COLOR: navy;");
txtstream->WriteLine("   FONT-FAMILY: font-family: Cambria, serif;");
txtstream->WriteLine("   FONT-SIZE: 12px;");
txtstream->WriteLine("   text-align: left;");
txtstream->WriteLine("   display: table-cell;");
txtstream->WriteLine("   white-Space: nowrap='nowrap';");
txtstream->WriteLine("   width: 100%;");
txtstream->WriteLine("}");
txtstream->WriteLine("h1 {");
txtstream->WriteLine("color: antiquewhite;");
txtstream->WriteLine("text-shadow: 1px 1px 1px black;");
txtstream->WriteLine("padding: 3px;");
txtstream->WriteLine("text-align: center;");
txtstream->WriteLine("box-shadow: inset 2px 2px 5px rgba(0,0,0,0->5), inset -
2px -2px 5px rgba(255,255,255,0->5);");
txtstream->WriteLine("}");
txtstream->WriteLine("</style>");
txtstream->WriteLine("<body>");
txtstream->WriteLine("<center>");
txtstream->WriteLine("</br>");
txtstream->WriteLine("</br>");
txtstream->WriteLine("<table border=0 cellspacing=3 cellpadding=3>");
txtstream->WriteLine("<tr>");
for each(System::Data::DataColumn^ col in dv->Table->Columns)
{
    txtstream->WriteLine("<th align='left' nowrap='nowrap'>" + col->Caption +
"</th>");
}
txtstream->WriteLine("</tr>");

for each(System::Data::DataRow^ dr in dv->Table->Rows)
{
```

```cpp
        txtstream->WriteLine("<tr>");
        for each(System::Data::DataColumn^ col in dv->Table->Columns)
        {
            txtstream->WriteLine("<td  align='left' nowrap='true'><input type=text
value=\"" + dr[col->Caption]->ToString() + \""></input></td>");
        }
        txtstream->WriteLine("</tr>");
    }
    txtstream->WriteLine("</table>");
    txtstream->WriteLine("</body>");
    txtstream->WriteLine("</html>");
    txtstream->Close();
```

A LOT OF CODE TO COVER

Overview

THERE IS A LOT OF CODE TO COVER AND, HONESTLY, I HATE INTRODUCTIONS. So, let's make this short and sweet. We're using OLEDB and the DataView to create outputs that include ASP, ASPX, Delimited Text Files, Excel, HTA, HTML, XML, and XSL. There, I said it, I'm done. From the OleDb coding perspective, use the following:

```
System::String^ cnstr = "";
System::String^ strQuery = "";
```

Connection, Command and DataAdapter

```
System::Data::OleDb::OleDbConnection^ cn = gcnew
System::Data::OleDb::OleDbConnection();
Cn->ConnectionString = cnstr;
Cn->Open();

System::Data::OleDb::OleDbCommand^ cmd = gcnew
System::Data::OleDb::OleDbCommand();
```

```
cmd->Connection = cn;
cmd->CommandType = System::Data::CommandType::Text;
cmd->CommandText = strQuery;
cmd->ExecuteNonquery();

System::Data::OleDb::OleDbDataAdapter^ da = gcnew
System::Data::OleDb::OleDbDataAdapter(cmd);

System::Data::DataTable^ dt = gcnewSystem::Data::DataTable;
da->Fill(dt);
System::Data::DataView^ dv = dt->DefaultView;
```

Connection and DataAdapter

```
System::Data::OleDb::OleDbConnection^ cn = gcnew
System::Data::OleDb::OleDbConnection();
Cn->ConnectionString = cnstr;
Cn->Open();

System::Data::OleDb::OleDbDataAdapter^ da = gcnew
System::Data::OleDb::OleDbDataAdapter(strQuery, cn);

System::Data::DataTable^ dt = gcnewSystem::Data::DataTable;
da->Fill(dt);
System::Data::DataView^ dv = dt->DefaultView;
```

Command and DataAdapter

```
System::Data::OleDb::OleDbCommand^ cmd = gcnew
System::Data::OleDb::OleDbCommand();
cmd->Connection = gcnew System::Data::OleDb::OleDbConnection;
cmd->Connection->ConnectionString = cnstr;")
cmd->Connection->Open();

cmd->CommandType = System::Data::CommandType::Text;
cmd->CommandText = strQuery;
cmd->ExecuteNonQuery();

System::Data::OleDb::OleDbDataAdapter^ da = gcnew
System::Data::OleDb::OleDbDataAdapter(cmd);

System::Data::DataTable^ dt = gcnewSystem::Data::DataTable;
da->Fill(dt);
System::Data::DataView^ dv = dt->DefaultView;
```

DataAdapter

```
System::Data::OleDb::OleDbDataAdapter^ da = gcnew
System::Data::OleDb::OleDbDataAdapter(strQuery, cnstr);

System::Data::DataTable^ dt = gcnewSystem::Data::DataTable;
da->Fill(dt);
System::Data::DataView^ dv = dt->DefaultView;
```

You are going to need to add one of the above ways to populate the dataadapter to the routines you plan on using.

ASP EXAMPLES

Let's do it!

B elow, are examples of using OLEDB, the DataView and ASP. And just in case you are wondering, I use none as meaning no additional tags between the <td></td>.

HORIZONTAL

```
Scripting::FileSystemObject^ fso = gcnew Scripting::FileSystemObject();
Scripting::TextStream^ txtstream = fso->OpenTextFile(Application::StartupPath +
"\\Products.asp",Scripting::IOMode::ForWriting, true,
Scripting::Tristate::TristateUseDefault);
txtstream->WriteLine("<html>");
txtstream->WriteLine("<head>");
txtstream->WriteLine("<title>Products</title>");
txtstream->WriteLine("<body>");
```

For Reports:

```
txtstream->WriteLine("<table border=0 cellspacing=3 cellpadding=3>");
```

For Tables:

```
txtstream->WriteLine("<table border=1 cellspacing=3 cellpadding=3>");

txtstream->WriteLine("<%");
txtstream->WriteLine("Response->Write(\"<tr>\" & vbcrlf)");
for each(System::Data::DataColumn^ col in dv->Table->Columns)
```

```
    {
        txtstream->WriteLine("Response->Write(\"<th align='left'
nowrap='nowrap'>" +   col->Caption + "</th>\" & vbcrlf)");
    }
    txtstream->WriteLine("Response->Write(\"</tr>\" & vbcrlf)");
```

Additional Tags:

None

```
    for each(System::Data::DataRow^ dr in dv->Table->Rows)
    {
        txtstream->WriteLine("Response->Write(\"<tr>\" & vbcrlf)");
        for each(System::Data::DataColumn^ col in dv->Table->Columns)
        {
            txtstream->WriteLine("Response->Write(\"<td  align='left'
nowrap='nowrap'>" + dr[col->Caption]->ToString() + "</td>\" & vbcrlf)");
        }
        txtstream->WriteLine("Response->Write(\"</tr>\" & vbcrlf)");
    }
```

Button

```
    for each(System::Data::DataRow^ dr in dv->Table->Rows)
    {
        txtstream->WriteLine("Response->Write(\"<tr>\" & vbcrlf)");
        for each(System::Data::DataColumn^ col in dv->Table->Columns)
        {
            txtstream->WriteLine("Response->Write(\"<td  align='left'
nowrap='true'><button style='width:100%;' value ='" + dr[col->Caption]-
>ToString() + "'>" + dr[col->Caption]->ToString() + "</button></td>\" & vbcrlf)");
        }
        txtstream->WriteLine("Response->Write(\"</tr>\" & vbcrlf)");
    }
```

Combobox

```
    for each(System::Data::DataRow^ dr in dv->Table->Rows)
    {
        txtstream->WriteLine("Response->Write(\"<tr>\" & vbcrlf)");
        for each(System::Data::DataColumn^ col in dv->Table->Columns)
        {
            txtstream->WriteLine("Response->Write(\"<td  align='left'
nowrap='true'><select><option value = \"" + dr[col->Caption]->ToString() + \"'>"
+ dr[col->Caption]->ToString() + "</option></select></td>\" & vbcrlf)");
        }
        txtstream->WriteLine("Response->Write(\"</tr>\" & vbcrlf)");
```

```
        }
```

```
    for each(System::Data::DataRow^ dr in dv->Table->Rows)
    {
        txtstream->WriteLine("Response->Write(\"<tr>\" & vbcrlf)");
        for each(System::Data::DataColumn^ col in dv->Table->Columns)
        {
            txtstream->WriteLine("Response->Write(\"<td align='left'
nowrap='true'><div>" + dr[col->Caption]->ToString() + "</div></td>\" & vbcrlf)");
        }
        txtstream->WriteLine("Response->Write(\"</tr>\" & vbcrlf)");
    }
```

```
    for each(System::Data::DataRow^ dr in dv->Table->Rows)
    {
        txtstream->WriteLine("Response->Write(\"<tr>\" & vbcrlf)");
        for each(System::Data::DataColumn^ col in dv->Table->Columns)
        {
            txtstream->WriteLine("Response->Write(\"<td align='left'
nowrap='true'><a href='" + dr[col->Caption]->ToString() + "'>" + dr[col-
>Caption]->ToString() + "</a></td>\" & vbcrlf)");
        }
        txtstream->WriteLine("Response->Write(\"</tr>\" & vbcrlf)");
    }
```

```
    for each(System::Data::DataRow^ dr in dv->Table->Rows)
    {
        txtstream->WriteLine("Response->Write(\"<tr>\" & vbcrlf)");
        for each(System::Data::DataColumn^ col in dv->Table->Columns)
        {
            txtstream->WriteLine("Response->Write(\"<td align='left'
nowrap='true'><select multiple><option value = \"" + dr[col->Caption]->ToString()
+ \""">" + dr[col->Caption]->ToString() + "</option></select></td>\" & vbcrlf)");
        }
        txtstream->WriteLine("Response->Write(\"</tr>\" & vbcrlf)");
    }
```

```
    for each(System::Data::DataRow^ dr in dv->Table->Rows)
```

```
    {
        txtstream->WriteLine("Response->Write(\"<tr>\" & vbcrlf)");
        for each(System::Data::DataColumn^ col in dv->Table->Columns)
        {
            txtstream->WriteLine("Response->Write(\"<td  align='left'
nowrap='true'><span>" + dr[col->Caption]->ToString() + "</span></td>\" &
vbcrlf)");
        }
        txtstream->WriteLine("Response->Write(\"</tr>\" & vbcrlf)");
    }
```

```
    for each(System::Data::DataRow^ dr in dv->Table->Rows)
    {
        txtstream->WriteLine("Response->Write(\"<tr>\" & vbcrlf)");
        for each(System::Data::DataColumn^ col in dv->Table->Columns)
        {
            txtstream->WriteLine("Response->Write(\"<td align='left'
nowrap='true'><textarea>" + dr[col->Caption]->ToString() + "</textarea></td>\"
& vbcrlf)");
        }
        txtstream->WriteLine("Response->Write(\"</tr>\" & vbcrlf)");
    }
```

```
    for each(System::Data::DataRow^ dr in dv->Table->Rows)
    {
        txtstream->WriteLine("Response->Write(\"<tr>\" & vbcrlf)");
        for each(System::Data::DataColumn^ col in dv->Table->Columns)
        {
            txtstream->WriteLine("Response->Write(\"<td  align='left'
nowrap='true'><input type=text value=\"" + dr[col->Caption]->ToString() +
\""></input></td>\" & vbcrlf)");
        }
        txtstream->WriteLine("Response->Write(\"</tr>\" & vbcrlf)");
    }
```

```
    txtstream->WriteLine("%>");
    txtstream->WriteLine("</table>");
    txtstream->WriteLine("</body>");
    txtstream->WriteLine("</html>");
    txtstream->Close();
```

VERTICAL

```
Scripting::FileSystemObject^ fso = gcnew Scripting::FileSystemObject();
Scripting::TextStream^ txtstream = fso->OpenTextFile(Application::StartupPath +
"\\Products.asp",Scripting::IOMode::ForWriting, true,
Scripting::Tristate::TristateUseDefault);
    txtstream->WriteLine("<html>");
    txtstream->WriteLine("<head>");
    txtstream->WriteLine("<title>Products</title>");
    txtstream->WriteLine("<body>");
    txtstream->WriteLine("<center>");
    txtstream->WriteLine("</br>");
    txtstream->WriteLine("</br>");
```

For Reports:

```
    txtstream->WriteLine("<table border=0 cellspacing=3 cellpadding=3>");
```

For Tables:

```
    txtstream->WriteLine("<table border=1 cellspacing=3 cellpadding=3>");

    txtstream->WriteLine("<%");
    for each(System::Data::DataColumn^ col in dv->Table->Columns)
    {
        txtstream->WriteLine("Response->Write(\"<tr><th align='left'
nowrap='nowrap'>" + col->Caption + "</th>\" & vbcrlf)");
```

None

```
    for each(System::Data::DataRow^ dr in dv->Table->Rows)
    {
        txtstream->WriteLine("Response->Write(\"<td  align='left'
nowrap='nowrap'>" + dr[col->Caption]->ToString() + "</td>\" & vbcrlf)");
    }
```

Additional Tags:

None

```
    for each(System::Data::DataRow^ dr in dv->Table->Rows)
    {
```

```
        txtstream->WriteLine("Response->Write(\"<td align='left'
nowrap='nowrap'>" + dr[col->Caption]->ToString() + "</td>\" & vbcrlf)");
        }
```

Button

```
      for each(System::Data::DataRow^ dr in dv->Table->Rows)
        {
        txtstream->WriteLine("Response->Write(\"<td align='left'
nowrap='true'><button style='width:100%;' value ='" + dr[col->Caption]-
>ToString() + "'>" + dr[col->Caption]->ToString() + "</button></td>\" & vbcrlf)");
        }
```

Combobox

```
      for each(System::Data::DataRow^ dr in dv->Table->Rows)
        {
        txtstream->WriteLine("Response->Write(\"<td align='left'
nowrap='true'><select><option value = \"" + dr[col->Caption]->ToString() + \"">"
+ dr[col->Caption]->ToString() + "</option></select></td>\" & vbcrlf)");
        }
```

Div

```
      for each(System::Data::DataRow^ dr in dv->Table->Rows)
        {
        txtstream->WriteLine("Response->Write(\"<td align='left'
nowrap='true'><div>" + dr[col->Caption]->ToString() + "</div></td>\" & vbcrlf)");
        }
```

Link

```
      for each(System::Data::DataRow^ dr in dv->Table->Rows)
        {
        txtstream->WriteLine("Response->Write(\"<td align='left'
nowrap='true'><a href='" + dr[col->Caption]->ToString() + "'>" + dr[col-
>Caption]->ToString() + "</a></td>\" & vbcrlf)");
        }
```

Listbox

```
      for each(System::Data::DataRow^ dr in dv->Table->Rows)
        {
        txtstream->WriteLine("Response->Write(\"<td align='left'
nowrap='true'><select multiple><option value = \"" + dr[col->Caption]->ToString()
+ \"">" + dr[col->Caption]->ToString() + "</option></select></td>\" & vbcrlf)");
```

```
    }
```

```
    for each(System::Data::DataRow^ dr in dv->Table->Rows)
    {
        txtstream->WriteLine("Response->Write(\"<td  align='left'
nowrap='true'><span>" + dr[col->Caption]->ToString() + "</span></td>\" &
vbcrlf)");
    }
```

```
    for each(System::Data::DataRow^ dr in dv->Table->Rows)
    {
        txtstream->WriteLine("Response->Write(\"<td  align='left'
nowrap='true'><textarea>" + dr[col->Caption]->ToString() + "</textarea></td>\"
& vbcrlf)");
    }
```

```
    for each(System::Data::DataRow^ dr in dv->Table->Rows)
    {
        txtstream->WriteLine("Response->Write(\"<td  align='left'
nowrap='true'><input type=text value=\"" + dr[col->Caption]->ToString() +
\""></input></td>\" & vbcrlf)");
    }
```

```
    txtstream->WriteLine("Response->Write(\"</tr>\" & vbcrlf)");
    }
    txtstream->WriteLine("%>");
    txtstream->WriteLine("</table>");
    txtstream->WriteLine("</body>");
    txtstream->WriteLine("</html>");
    txtstream->Close();
```

ASPX EXAMPLES

Yes, you can!

Below, are examples of using OLEDB, the DataView and ASPX. And just in case you are wondering, I use none as meaning no additional tags between the <td></td>

HORIZONTAL

```
Scripting::FileSystemObject^ fso = gcnew Scripting::FileSystemObject();
Scripting::TextStream^ txtstream = fso->OpenTextFile(Application::StartupPath +
"\\Products.asp",Scripting::IOMode::ForWriting, true,
Scripting::Tristate::TristateUseDefault);
   txtstream->WriteLine("<html>");
   txtstream->WriteLine("<head>");
   txtstream->WriteLine("<title>Products</title>");
   txtstream->WriteLine("<body>");
```

For Reports:

```
   txtstream->WriteLine("<table border=0 cellspacing=3 cellpadding=3>");
```

For Tables:

```
   txtstream->WriteLine("<table border=1 cellspacing=3 cellpadding=3>");

   txtstream->WriteLine("<%");
```

```
txtstream->WriteLine("Response->Write(\"<tr>\" & vbcrlf)");
for each(System::Data::DataColumn^ col in dv->Table->Columns)
{
    txtstream->WriteLine("Response->Write(\"<th align='left'
nowrap='nowrap'>" +   col->Caption + "</th>\" & vbcrlf)");
}
txtstream->WriteLine("Response->Write(\"</tr>\" & vbcrlf)");
```

Additional Tags:

None

```
for each(System::Data::DataRow^ dr in dv->Table->Rows)
{
    txtstream->WriteLine("Response->Write(\"<tr>\" & vbcrlf)");
    for each(System::Data::DataColumn^ col in dv->Table->Columns)
    {
        txtstream->WriteLine("Response->Write(\"<td align='left'
nowrap='nowrap'>" + dr[col->Caption]->ToString() + "</td>\" & vbcrlf)");
    }
    txtstream->WriteLine("Response->Write(\"</tr>\" & vbcrlf)");
}
```

Button

```
for each(System::Data::DataRow^ dr in dv->Table->Rows)
{
    txtstream->WriteLine("Response->Write(\"<tr>\" & vbcrlf)");
    for each(System::Data::DataColumn^ col in dv->Table->Columns)
    {
        txtstream->WriteLine("Response->Write(\"<td align='left'
nowrap='true'><button style='width:100%;' value ='" + dr[col->Caption]-
>ToString() + "'>" + dr[col->Caption]->ToString() + "</button></td>\" & vbcrlf)");
    }
    txtstream->WriteLine("Response->Write(\"</tr>\" & vbcrlf)");
}
```

Combobox

```
for each(System::Data::DataRow^ dr in dv->Table->Rows)
{
    txtstream->WriteLine("Response->Write(\"<tr>\" & vbcrlf)");
    for each(System::Data::DataColumn^ col in dv->Table->Columns)
    {
        txtstream->WriteLine("Response->Write(\"<td align='left'
nowrap='true'><select><option value = \"" + dr[col->Caption]->ToString() + "'">"
+ dr[col->Caption]->ToString() + "</option></select></td>\" & vbcrlf)");
```

```
        }
        txtstream->WriteLine("Response->Write(\"</tr>\" & vbcrlf)");
    }
```

```
    for each(System::Data::DataRow^ dr in dv->Table->Rows)
    {
        txtstream->WriteLine("Response->Write(\"<tr>\" & vbcrlf)");
        for each(System::Data::DataColumn^ col in dv->Table->Columns)
        {
            txtstream->WriteLine("Response->Write(\"<td align='left'
nowrap='true'><div>" + dr[col->Caption]->ToString() + "</div></td>\" & vbcrlf)");
        }
        txtstream->WriteLine("Response->Write(\"</tr>\" & vbcrlf)");
    }
```

```
    for each(System::Data::DataRow^ dr in dv->Table->Rows)
    {
        txtstream->WriteLine("Response->Write(\"<tr>\" & vbcrlf)");
        for each(System::Data::DataColumn^ col in dv->Table->Columns)
        {
            txtstream->WriteLine("Response->Write(\"<td align='left'
nowrap='true'><a href='" + dr[col->Caption]->ToString() + "'>" + dr[col-
>Caption]->ToString() + "</a></td>\" & vbcrlf)");
        }
        txtstream->WriteLine("Response->Write(\"</tr>\" & vbcrlf)");
    }
```

```
    for each(System::Data::DataRow^ dr in dv->Table->Rows)
    {
        txtstream->WriteLine("Response->Write(\"<tr>\" & vbcrlf)");
        for each(System::Data::DataColumn^ col in dv->Table->Columns)
        {
            txtstream->WriteLine("Response->Write(\"<td align='left'
nowrap='true'><select multiple><option value = \"" + dr[col->Caption]->ToString()
+ \"">" + dr[col->Caption]->ToString() + "</option></select></td>\" & vbcrlf)");
        }
        txtstream->WriteLine("Response->Write(\"</tr>\" & vbcrlf)");
    }
```

```
for each(System::Data::DataRow^ dr in dv->Table->Rows)
{
    txtstream->WriteLine("Response->Write(\"<tr>\" & vbcrlf)");
    for each(System::Data::DataColumn^ col in dv->Table->Columns)
    {
        txtstream->WriteLine("Response->Write(\"<td align='left'
nowrap='true'><span>" + dr[col->Caption]->ToString() + "</span></td>\" &
vbcrlf)");
    }
    txtstream->WriteLine("Response->Write(\"</tr>\" & vbcrlf)");
}
```

Textarea

```
for each(System::Data::DataRow^ dr in dv->Table->Rows)
{
    txtstream->WriteLine("Response->Write(\"<tr>\" & vbcrlf)");
    for each(System::Data::DataColumn^ col in dv->Table->Columns)
    {
        txtstream->WriteLine("Response->Write(\"<td  align='left'
nowrap='true'><textarea>" + dr[col->Caption]->ToString() + "</textarea></td>\"
& vbcrlf)");
    }
    txtstream->WriteLine("Response->Write(\"</tr>\" & vbcrlf)");
}
```
Textbox

```
for each(System::Data::DataRow^ dr in dv->Table->Rows)
{
    txtstream->WriteLine("Response->Write(\"<tr>\" & vbcrlf)");
    for each(System::Data::DataColumn^ col in dv->Table->Columns)
    {
        txtstream->WriteLine("Response->Write(\"<td  align='left'
nowrap='true'><input type=text value=\"" + dr[col->Caption]->ToString() +
\"" ></input></td>\" & vbcrlf)");
    }
    txtstream->WriteLine("Response->Write(\"</tr>\" & vbcrlf)");
}
```

End Code

```
txtstream->WriteLine("%>");
txtstream->WriteLine("</table>");
txtstream->WriteLine("</body>");
txtstream->WriteLine("</html>");
```

```
    txtstream->Close();
```

VERTICAL

```
    Scripting::FileSystemObject^ fso = gcnew Scripting::FileSystemObject();
    Scripting::TextStream^ txtstream = fso->OpenTextFile(Application::StartupPath +
"\\Products.asp",Scripting::IOMode::ForWriting, true,
Scripting::Tristate::TristateUseDefault);
    txtstream->WriteLine("<html>");
    txtstream->WriteLine("<head>");
    txtstream->WriteLine("<title>Products</title>");
    txtstream->WriteLine("<body>");
    txtstream->WriteLine("<center>");
    txtstream->WriteLine("</br>");
    txtstream->WriteLine("</br>");
```

For Reports:

```
    txtstream->WriteLine("<table border=0 cellspacing=3 cellpadding=3>");
```

For Tables:

```
    txtstream->WriteLine("<table border=1 cellspacing=3 cellpadding=3>");

    txtstream->WriteLine("<%");
    for each(System::Data::DataColumn^ col in dv->Table->Columns)
    {
        txtstream->WriteLine("Response->Write(\"<tr><th align='left'
nowrap='nowrap'>" + col->Caption + "</th>\" & vbcrlf)");
```

None

```
    for each(System::Data::DataRow^ dr in dv->Table->Rows)
    {
        txtstream->WriteLine("Response->Write(\"<td align='left'
nowrap='nowrap'>" + dr[col->Caption]->ToString() + "</td>\" & vbcrlf)");
    }
```

Additional Tags:

```
for each(System::Data::DataRow^ dr in dv->Table->Rows)
{
    txtstream->WriteLine("Response->Write(\"<td align='left'
nowrap='nowrap'>" + dr[col->Caption]->ToString() + "</td>\" & vbcrlf)");
}
```

Button

```
for each(System::Data::DataRow^ dr in dv->Table->Rows)
{
    txtstream->WriteLine("Response->Write(\"<td  align='left'
nowrap='true'><button style='width:100%;' value ='" + dr[col->Caption]-
>ToString() + "'>" + dr[col->Caption]->ToString() + "</button></td>\" & vbcrlf)");
}
```

Combobox

```
for each(System::Data::DataRow^ dr in dv->Table->Rows)
{
    txtstream->WriteLine("Response->Write(\"<td  align='left'
nowrap='true'><select><option value = \"" + dr[col->Caption]->ToString() + \""'>"
+ dr[col->Caption]->ToString() + "</option></select></td>\" & vbcrlf)");
}
```

Div

```
for each(System::Data::DataRow^ dr in dv->Table->Rows)
{
    txtstream->WriteLine("Response->Write(\"<td  align='left'
nowrap='true'><div>" + dr[col->Caption]->ToString() + "</div></td>\" & vbcrlf)");
}
```

Link

```
for each(System::Data::DataRow^ dr in dv->Table->Rows)
{
    txtstream->WriteLine("Response->Write(\"<td  align='left'
nowrap='true'><a href='" + dr[col->Caption]->ToString() + "'>" + dr[col-
>Caption]->ToString() + "</a></td>\" & vbcrlf)");
}
```

Listbox

```cpp
    for each(System::Data::DataRow^ dr in dv->Table->Rows)
    {
        txtstream->WriteLine("Response->Write(\"<td align='left'
nowrap='true'><select multiple><option value = \"" + dr[col->Caption]->ToString()
+ \"">" + dr[col->Caption]->ToString() + "</option></select></td>\" & vbcrlf)");
    }
```

Span

```cpp
    for each(System::Data::DataRow^ dr in dv->Table->Rows)
    {
        txtstream->WriteLine("Response->Write(\"<td align='left'
nowrap='true'><span>" + dr[col->Caption]->ToString() + "</span></td>\" &
vbcrlf)");
    }
```

Textarea

```cpp
    for each(System::Data::DataRow^ dr in dv->Table->Rows)
    {
        txtstream->WriteLine("Response->Write(\"<td  align='left'
nowrap='true'><textarea>" + dr[col->Caption]->ToString() + "</textarea></td>\"
& vbcrlf)");
    }
```

Textbox

```cpp
    for each(System::Data::DataRow^ dr in dv->Table->Rows)
    {
        txtstream->WriteLine("Response->Write(\"<td align='left'
nowrap='true'><input type=text value=\"" + dr[col->Caption]->ToString() +
\"" ></input></td>\" & vbcrlf)");
    }
```

End Code

```cpp
    txtstream->WriteLine("Response->Write(\"</tr>\" & vbcrlf)");
}
txtstream->WriteLine("%>");
txtstream->WriteLine("</table>");
txtstream->WriteLine("</body>");
txtstream->WriteLine("</html>");
txtstream->Close();
```

HTA EXAMPLES

Let's do it!

B elow, are examples of using OLEDB, the DataView and ASP. And just in case you are wondering, I use none as meaning no additional tags between the <td></td>.

HORIZONTAL

```
Scripting::FileSystemObject^ fso = gcnew Scripting::FileSystemObject();
Scripting::TextStream^ txtstream = fso->OpenTextFile(Application::StartupPath +
"\\Products.asp",Scripting::IOMode::ForWriting, true,
Scripting::Tristate::TristateUseDefault);
    txtstream->WriteLine("<html>");
    txtstream->WriteLine("<head>");
    txtstream->WriteLine("<HTA:APPLICATION ");
    txtstream->WriteLine("ID = 'Products' ");
    txtstream->WriteLine("APPLICATIONNAME = 'Products' ");
    txtstream->WriteLine("SCROLL = 'yes' ");
    txtstream->WriteLine("SINGLEINSTANCE = 'yes' ");
    txtstream->WriteLine("WINDOWSTATE = 'maximize' >");
    txtstream->WriteLine("<title>Products</title>");
    txtstream->WriteLine("<body>");
```

For Reports:

```
txtstream->WriteLine("<table border=0 cellspacing=3 cellpadding=3>");
```

For Tables:

```
txtstream->WriteLine("<table border=1 cellspacing=3 cellpadding=3>");

txtstream->WriteLine("<tr>");
for each(System::Data::DataColumn^ col in dv->Table->Columns)
{
    txtstream->WriteLine("<th align='left' nowrap='nowrap'>" +   col->Caption +
"</th>");
}
txtstream->WriteLine("</tr>");
```

Additional Tags:

None

```
for each(System::Data::DataRow^ dr in dv->Table->Rows)
{
    txtstream->WriteLine("<tr>");
    for each(System::Data::DataColumn^ col in dv->Table->Columns)
    {
        txtstream->WriteLine("<td  align='left' nowrap='nowrap'>" + dr[col-
>Caption]->ToString() + "</td>");
    }
    txtstream->WriteLine("</tr>");
}
```

Button

```
for each(System::Data::DataRow^ dr in dv->Table->Rows)
{
    txtstream->WriteLine("<tr>");
    for each(System::Data::DataColumn^ col in dv->Table->Columns)
    {
        txtstream->WriteLine("<td  align='left' nowrap='true'><button
style='width:100%;' value ='" + dr[col->Caption]->ToString() + "'>" + dr[col-
>Caption]->ToString() + "</button></td>");
    }
    txtstream->WriteLine("</tr>");
}
```

Combobox

```
for each(System::Data::DataRow^ dr in dv->Table->Rows)
{
```

```cpp
        txtstream->WriteLine("<tr>");
        for each(System::Data::DataColumn^ col in dv->Table->Columns)
        {
            txtstream->WriteLine("<td align='left' nowrap='true'><select><option
value = \"" + dr[col->Caption]->ToString() + \"">" + dr[col->Caption]->ToString()
+ "</option></select></td>");
        }
        txtstream->WriteLine("</tr>");
    }
```

Div

```cpp
    for each(System::Data::DataRow^ dr in dv->Table->Rows)
    {
        txtstream->WriteLine("<tr>");
        for each(System::Data::DataColumn^ col in dv->Table->Columns)
        {
            txtstream->WriteLine("<td align='left' nowrap='true'><div>" + dr[col-
>Caption]->ToString() + "</div></td>");
        }
        txtstream->WriteLine("</tr>");
    }
```

Link

```cpp
    for each(System::Data::DataRow^ dr in dv->Table->Rows)
    {
        txtstream->WriteLine("<tr>");
        for each(System::Data::DataColumn^ col in dv->Table->Columns)
        {
            txtstream->WriteLine("<td align='left' nowrap='true'><a href='" + dr[col-
>Caption]->ToString() + "'>" + dr[col->Caption]->ToString() + "</a></td>");
        }
        txtstream->WriteLine("</tr>");
    }
```

Listbox

```cpp
    for each(System::Data::DataRow^ dr in dv->Table->Rows)
    {
        txtstream->WriteLine("<tr>");
        for each(System::Data::DataColumn^ col in dv->Table->Columns)
        {
            txtstream->WriteLine("<td align='left' nowrap='true'><select
multiple><option value = \"" + dr[col->Caption]->ToString() + \"">" + dr[col-
>Caption]->ToString() + "</option></select></td>");
        }
```

```
    txtstream->WriteLine("</tr>");
  }
```

Span

```
  for each(System::Data::DataRow^ dr in dv->Table->Rows)
  {
    txtstream->WriteLine("<tr>");
    for each(System::Data::DataColumn^ col in dv->Table->Columns)
    {
      txtstream->WriteLine("<td align='left' nowrap='true'><span>" + dr[col
->Caption]->ToString() + "</span></td>");
    }
    txtstream->WriteLine("</tr>");
  }
```

Textarea

```
  for each(System::Data::DataRow^ dr in dv->Table->Rows)
  {
    txtstream->WriteLine("<tr>");
    for each(System::Data::DataColumn^ col in dv->Table->Columns)
    {
      txtstream->WriteLine("<td align='left' nowrap='true'><textarea>" + dr[col
->Caption]->ToString() + "</textarea></td>");
    }
    txtstream->WriteLine("</tr>");
  }
```
Textbox

```
  for each(System::Data::DataRow^ dr in dv->Table->Rows)
  {
    txtstream->WriteLine("<tr>");
    for each(System::Data::DataColumn^ col in dv->Table->Columns)
    {
      txtstream->WriteLine("<td align='left' nowrap='true'><input type=text
value=\"" + dr[col->Caption]->ToString() + \""></input></td>");
    }
    txtstream->WriteLine("</tr>");
  }
```

End Code

```
  txtstream->WriteLine("</table>");
  txtstream->WriteLine("</body>");
  txtstream->WriteLine("</html>");
```

```
txtstream->Close();
```

VERTICAL

```
Scripting::FileSystemObject^ fso = gcnew Scripting::FileSystemObject();
Scripting::TextStream^ txtstream = fso->OpenTextFile(Application::StartupPath +
"\\Products.asp",Scripting::IOMode::ForWriting, true,
Scripting::Tristate::TristateUseDefault);
txtstream->WriteLine("<html>");
txtstream->WriteLine("<head>");
txtstream->WriteLine("<title>Products</title>");
txtstream->WriteLine("<body>");
txtstream->WriteLine("<center>");
txtstream->WriteLine("</br>");
txtstream->WriteLine("</br>");
```

For Reports:

```
txtstream->WriteLine("<table border=0 cellspacing=3 cellpadding=3>");
```

For Tables:

```
txtstream->WriteLine("<table border=1 cellspacing=3 cellpadding=3>");

for each(System::Data::DataColumn^ col in dv->Table->Columns)
{
    txtstream->WriteLine("<tr><th align='left' nowrap='nowrap'>" + col->Caption
+ "</th>");
```

Additional Tags:

None

```
for each(System::Data::DataRow^ dr in dv->Table->Rows)
{
    txtstream->WriteLine("<td  align='left' nowrap='nowrap'>" + dr[col-
>Caption]->ToString() + "</td>");
}
```

Button

```
for each(System::Data::DataRow^ dr in dv->Table->Rows)
{
```

```
    txtstream->WriteLine("<td align='left' nowrap='true'><button
style='width:100%;' value ='" + dr[col->Caption]->ToString() + "'>" + dr[col-
>Caption]->ToString() + "</button></td>");
    }
```

Combobox

```
    for each(System::Data::DataRow^ dr in dv->Table->Rows)
    {
        txtstream->WriteLine("<td align='left' nowrap='true'><select><option
value = \"" + dr[col->Caption]->ToString() + \"">" + dr[col->Caption]->ToString()
+ "</option></select></td>");
    }
```

Div

```
    for each(System::Data::DataRow^ dr in dv->Table->Rows)
    {
        txtstream->WriteLine("<td align='left' nowrap='true'><div>" + dr[col-
>Caption]->ToString() + "</div></td>");
    }
```

Link

```
    for each(System::Data::DataRow^ dr in dv->Table->Rows)
    {
        txtstream->WriteLine("<td align='left' nowrap='true'><a href='" + dr[col-
>Caption]->ToString() + "'>" + dr[col->Caption]->ToString() + "</a></td>");
    }
```

Listbox

```
    for each(System::Data::DataRow^ dr in dv->Table->Rows)
    {
        txtstream->WriteLine("<td align='left' nowrap='true'><select
multiple><option value = \"" + dr[col->Caption]->ToString() + \"">" + dr[col-
>Caption]->ToString() + "</option></select></td>");
    }
```
Span

```
    for each(System::Data::DataRow^ dr in dv->Table->Rows)
    {
        txtstream->WriteLine("<td align='left' nowrap='true'><span>" + dr[col-
>Caption]->ToString() + "</span></td>");
    }
```

```
for each(System::Data::DataRow^ dr in dv->Table->Rows)
{
    txtstream->WriteLine("<td align='left' nowrap='true'><textarea>" + dr[col-
>Caption]->ToString() + "</textarea></td>");
}
```

Textbox

```
for each(System::Data::DataRow^ dr in dv->Table->Rows)
{
    txtstream->WriteLine("<td align='left' nowrap='true'><input type=text
value=\"" + dr[col->Caption]->ToString() + \""></input></td>");
}
```

End Code

```
    txtstream->WriteLine("</tr>");
}
txtstream->WriteLine("</table>");
txtstream->WriteLine("</body>");
txtstream->WriteLine("</html>");
txtstream->Close();
```

HTML EXAMPLES

Let's do it!

B elow, are examples of using OLEDB, the DataView and HTML. And just in case you are wondering, I use none as meaning no additional tags between the <td></td>.

HORIZONTAL

```
Scripting::FileSystemObject^ fso = gcnew Scripting::FileSystemObject();
Scripting::TextStream^ txtstream = fso->OpenTextFile(Application::StartupPath +
"\\Products.asp",Scripting::IOMode::ForWriting, true,
Scripting::Tristate::TristateUseDefault);
  txtstream->WriteLine("<html>");
  txtstream->WriteLine("<head>");
  txtstream->WriteLine("<title>Products</title>");
  txtstream->WriteLine("<body>");
```

For Reports:

```
  txtstream->WriteLine("<table border=0 cellspacing=3 cellpadding=3>");
```

For Tables:

```
  txtstream->WriteLine("<table border=1 cellspacing=3 cellpadding=3>");
```

```
    txtstream->WriteLine("<%");
    txtstream->WriteLine("<tr>");
    for each(System::Data::DataColumn^ col in dv->Table->Columns)
    {
        txtstream->WriteLine("<th align='left' nowrap='nowrap'>" +   col->Caption +
"</th>");
    }
    txtstream->WriteLine("</tr>");
```

Additional Tags:

None

```
    for each(System::Data::DataRow^ dr in dv->Table->Rows)
    {
        txtstream->WriteLine("<tr>");
        for each(System::Data::DataColumn^ col in dv->Table->Columns)
        {
            txtstream->WriteLine("<td  align='left' nowrap='nowrap'>" + dr[col-
>Caption]->ToString() + "</td>");
        }
        txtstream->WriteLine("</tr>");
    }
```

Button

```
    for each(System::Data::DataRow^ dr in dv->Table->Rows)
    {
        txtstream->WriteLine("<tr>");
        for each(System::Data::DataColumn^ col in dv->Table->Columns)
        {
            txtstream->WriteLine("<td  align='left' nowrap='true'><button
style='width:100%;' value ='" + dr[col->Caption]->ToString() + "'>" + dr[col-
>Caption]->ToString() + "</button></td>");
        }
        txtstream->WriteLine("</tr>");
    }
```

Combobox

```
    for each(System::Data::DataRow^ dr in dv->Table->Rows)
    {
        txtstream->WriteLine("<tr>");
        for each(System::Data::DataColumn^ col in dv->Table->Columns)
        {
```

```
        txtstream->WriteLine("<td align='left' nowrap='true'><select><option
value = \"'" + dr[col->Caption]->ToString() + \"'">" + dr[col->Caption]->ToString()
+ "</option></select></td>");
        }
        txtstream->WriteLine("</tr>");
    }
```

Div

```
    for each(System::Data::DataRow^ dr in dv->Table->Rows)
    {
        txtstream->WriteLine("<tr>");
        for each(System::Data::DataColumn^ col in dv->Table->Columns)
        {
            txtstream->WriteLine("<td align='left' nowrap='true'><div>" + dr[col-
>Caption]->ToString() + "</div></td>");
        }
        txtstream->WriteLine("</tr>");
    }
```

Link

```
    for each(System::Data::DataRow^ dr in dv->Table->Rows)
    {
        txtstream->WriteLine("<tr>");
        for each(System::Data::DataColumn^ col in dv->Table->Columns)
        {
            txtstream->WriteLine("<td align='left' nowrap='true'><a href='" + dr[col-
>Caption]->ToString() + "'>" + dr[col->Caption]->ToString() + "</a></td>");
        }
        txtstream->WriteLine("</tr>");
    }
```

Listbox

```
    for each(System::Data::DataRow^ dr in dv->Table->Rows)
    {
        txtstream->WriteLine("<tr>");
        for each(System::Data::DataColumn^ col in dv->Table->Columns)
        {
            txtstream->WriteLine("<td align='left' nowrap='true'><select
multiple><option value = \"'" + dr[col->Caption]->ToString() + \"'">" + dr[col-
>Caption]->ToString() + "</option></select></td>");
        }
        txtstream->WriteLine("</tr>");
    }
```

```cpp
for each(System::Data::DataRow^ dr in dv->Table->Rows)
{
    txtstream->WriteLine("<tr>");
    for each(System::Data::DataColumn^ col in dv->Table->Columns)
    {
        txtstream->WriteLine("<td align='left' nowrap='true'><span>" + dr[col->Caption]->ToString() + "</span></td>");
    }
    txtstream->WriteLine("</tr>");
}
```

Textarea

```cpp
for each(System::Data::DataRow^ dr in dv->Table->Rows)
{
    txtstream->WriteLine("<tr>");
    for each(System::Data::DataColumn^ col in dv->Table->Columns)
    {
        txtstream->WriteLine("<td  align='left' nowrap='true'><textarea>" + dr[col->Caption]->ToString() + "</textarea></td>");
    }
    txtstream->WriteLine("</tr>");
}
```

Textbox

```cpp
for each(System::Data::DataRow^ dr in dv->Table->Rows)
{
    txtstream->WriteLine("<tr>");
    for each(System::Data::DataColumn^ col in dv->Table->Columns)
    {
        txtstream->WriteLine("<td  align='left' nowrap='true'><input type=text value=\"" + dr[col->Caption]->ToString() + "\"></input></td>");
    }
    txtstream->WriteLine("</tr>");
}
```

End Code

```cpp
txtstream->WriteLine("%>");
txtstream->WriteLine("</table>");
txtstream->WriteLine("</body>");
txtstream->WriteLine("</html>");
txtstream->Close();
```

VERTICAL

```
Scripting::FileSystemObject^ fso = gcnew Scripting::FileSystemObject();
Scripting::TextStream^ txtstream = fso->OpenTextFile(Application::StartupPath +
"\\Products.asp",Scripting::IOMode::ForWriting, true,
Scripting::Tristate::TristateUseDefault);
txtstream->WriteLine("<html>");
txtstream->WriteLine("<head>");
txtstream->WriteLine("<title>Products</title>");
txtstream->WriteLine("<body>");
txtstream->WriteLine("<center>");
txtstream->WriteLine("</br>");
txtstream->WriteLine("</br>");
```

For Reports:

```
txtstream->WriteLine("<table border=0 cellspacing=3 cellpadding=3>");
```

For Tables:

```
txtstream->WriteLine("<table border=1 cellspacing=3 cellpadding=3>");

for each(System::Data::DataColumn^ col in dv->Table->Columns)
{
    txtstream->WriteLine("<tr><th align='left' nowrap='nowrap'>" + col->Caption
+ "</th>");
```

Additional Tags:

None

```
for each(System::Data::DataRow^ dr in dv->Table->Rows)
{
    txtstream->WriteLine("<td align='left' nowrap='nowrap'>" + dr[col-
>Caption]->ToString() + "</td>");
}
```

Button

```
for each(System::Data::DataRow^ dr in dv->Table->Rows)
{
    txtstream->WriteLine("<td align='left' nowrap='true'><button
style='width:100%;' value ='" + dr[col->Caption]->ToString() + "'>" + dr[col-
>Caption]->ToString() + "</button></td>");
```

```
            }
```

```
        for each(System::Data::DataRow^ dr in dv->Table->Rows)
        {
            txtstream->WriteLine("<td align='left' nowrap='true'><select><option
value = \"" + dr[col->Caption]->ToString() + \"">" + dr[col->Caption]->ToString()
+ "</option></select></td>");
        }
```

Div

```
        for each(System::Data::DataRow^ dr in dv->Table->Rows)
        {
            txtstream->WriteLine("<td align='left' nowrap='true'><div>" + dr[col-
>Caption]->ToString() + "</div></td>");
        }
```

Link

```
        for each(System::Data::DataRow^ dr in dv->Table->Rows)
        {
            txtstream->WriteLine("<td align='left' nowrap='true'><a href='" + dr[col-
>Caption]->ToString() + "'>" + dr[col->Caption]->ToString() + "</a></td>");
        }
```

Listbox

```
        for each(System::Data::DataRow^ dr in dv->Table->Rows)
        {
            txtstream->WriteLine("<td align='left' nowrap='true'><select
multiple><option value = \"" + dr[col->Caption]->ToString() + \"">" + dr[col-
>Caption]->ToString() + "</option></select></td>");
        }
```

Span

```
        for each(System::Data::DataRow^ dr in dv->Table->Rows)
        {
            txtstream->WriteLine("<td align='left' nowrap='true'><span>" + dr[col-
>Caption]->ToString() + "</span></td>");
        }
```

Textarea

```
for each(System::Data::DataRow^ dr in dv->Table->Rows)
{
    txtstream->WriteLine("<td align='left' nowrap='true'><textarea>" + dr[col-
>Caption]->ToString() + "</textarea></td>");
}
```

Textbox

```
for each(System::Data::DataRow^ dr in dv->Table->Rows)
{
    txtstream->WriteLine("<td align='left' nowrap='true'><input type=text
value=\"" + dr[col->Caption]->ToString() + \""></input></td>");
}
```

End Code

```
    txtstream->WriteLine("</tr>");
}
txtstream->WriteLine("</table>");
txtstream->WriteLine("</body>");
txtstream->WriteLine("</html>");
txtstream->Close();
```

DELIMITED TEXT FILES

B ELOW ARE THE POPULAR EXAMPLES OF DIFFERENT DELIMITED TEXT
FILES.

COLON DELIMITED HORIZONTAL VIEW

```
System::String^ tempstr = "";

Scripting::FileSystemObject^ fso = gcnew Scripting::FileSystemObject();
Scripting::TextStream^ txtstream = fso->OpenTextFile(Application::StartupPath +
"\Products->txt",Scripting::IOMode::ForWriting, true,
Scripting::Tristate::TristateUseDefault);
for each(System::Data::DataColumn^ col in dv->Table->Columns)
{
   if (tempstr != "")
   {
      tempstr = tempstr + ":";
   }
   tempstr = tempstr + col->Caption;
}
txtstream->WriteLine(tempstr);
tempstr = "";

foreach(System::Data::DataRow^ dr in dv->Table->rows)
{
   for each(System::Data::DataColumn^ col in dv->Table->Columns)
   {
      if (tempstr != "")
      {
```

```
        tempstr = tempstr + ":";
    }
        tempstr = tempstr + "\\" + dr[col->Caption]->ToString() + "\\";
    }
    txtstream->WriteLine(tempstr);
    tempstr = "";

}
txtstream->Close();
```

COLON DELIMITED VERTICAL VIEW

```
System::String^ tempstr = "";

Scripting::FileSystemObject^ fso = gcnew Scripting::FileSystemObject();
Scripting::TextStream^ txtstream = fso->OpenTextFile(Application::StartupPath +
"\Products->txt",Scripting::IOMode::ForWriting, true,
Scripting::Tristate::TristateUseDefault);
for each(System::Data::DataColumn^ col in dv->Table->Columns)
{
    tempstr = col->Caption;
    foreach(System::Data::DataRow^ dr in dv->Table->rows)
    {
        if (tempstr != "")
        {
            tempstr = tempstr + ":";
        }
            tempstr = tempstr + "\\" + dr[col->Caption]->ToString() + "\\";
    }
    txtstream->WriteLine(tempstr);
    tempstr = "";

}
txtstream->Close();
```

COMMA DELIMITED HORIZONTAL VIEW

```
System::String^ tempstr = "";

Scripting::FileSystemObject^ fso = gcnew Scripting::FileSystemObject();
Scripting::TextStream^ txtstream = fso->OpenTextFile(Application::StartupPath +
"\Products->csv",Scripting::IOMode::ForWriting, true,
Scripting::Tristate::TristateUseDefault);
for each(System::Data::DataColumn^ col in dv->Table->Columns)
```

```
{
   if (tempstr != """)
   {
      tempstr = tempstr + ",";
   }
   tempstr = tempstr + col->Caption;
}
txtstream->WriteLine(tempstr);
tempstr = """;

foreach(System::Data::DataRow^ dr in dv->Table->rows)
{
   for each(System::Data::DataColumn^ col in dv->Table->Columns)
   {
      if (tempstr != """)
      {
         tempstr = tempstr + ",";
      }
         tempstr = tempstr + "\\" + dr[col->Caption]->ToString() + "\\";
   }
   txtstream->WriteLine(tempstr);
   tempstr = """;

}
txtstream->Close();
```

COMMA DELIMITED VERTICAL VIEW

```
System::String^ tempstr = """;

Scripting::FileSystemObject^ fso = gcnew Scripting::FileSystemObject();
Scripting::TextStream^ txtstream = fso->OpenTextFile(Application::StartupPath +
"\Products->csv",Scripting::IOMode::ForWriting, true,
Scripting::Tristate::TristateUseDefault);
for each(System::Data::DataColumn^ col in dv->Table->Columns)
{
   tempstr = col->Caption;
   foreach(System::Data::DataRow^ dr in dv->Table->rows)
   {
      if (tempstr != """)
      {
         tempstr = tempstr + ",";
      }
         tempstr = tempstr + "\\" + dr[col->Caption]->ToString() + "\\";
   }
}
   txtstream->WriteLine(tempstr);
```

```
      tempstr = "";

}
txtstream->Close();
```

EXCLAMATION DELIMITED HORIZONTAL VIEW

```
System::String^ tempstr = "";

Scripting::FileSystemObject^ fso = gcnew Scripting::FileSystemObject();
Scripting::TextStream^ txtstream = fso->OpenTextFile(Application::StartupPath +
"\Products->txt",Scripting::IOMode::ForWriting, true,
Scripting::Tristate::TristateUseDefault);
for each(System::Data::DataColumn^ col in dv->Table->Columns)
{
   if (tempstr != "")
   {
      tempstr = tempstr + "!";
   }
   tempstr = tempstr + col->Caption;
}
txtstream->WriteLine(tempstr);
tempstr = "";

foreach(System::Data::DataRow^ dr in dv->Table->rows)
{
   for each(System::Data::DataColumn^ col in dv->Table->Columns)
   {
      if (tempstr != "")
      {
         tempstr = tempstr + "!";
      }
      tempstr = tempstr + "\\" + dr[col->Caption]->ToString() + "\\";
   }
   txtstream->WriteLine(tempstr);
   tempstr = "";

}
txtstream->Close();
```

EXCLAMATION DELIMITED VERTICAL VIEW

```
System::String^ tempstr = "";
```

```
Scripting::FileSystemObject^ fso = gcnew Scripting::FileSystemObject();
Scripting::TextStream^ txtstream = fso->OpenTextFile(Application::StartupPath +
"\Products->txt",Scripting::IOMode::ForWriting, true,
Scripting::Tristate::TristateUseDefault);
for each(System::Data::DataColumn^ col in dv->Table->Columns)
{
    tempstr = col->Caption;
    foreach(System::Data::DataRow^ dr in dv->Table->rows)
    {
        if (tempstr != "")
        {
            tempstr = tempstr + "!";
        }
            tempstr = tempstr + "\\" + dr[col->Caption]->ToString() + "\\";
        }
    }
    txtstream->WriteLine(tempstr);
    tempstr = "";

}
txtstream->Close();
```

SEMI-COLON DELIMITED HORIZONTAL VIEW

```
System::String^ tempstr = "";

Scripting::FileSystemObject^ fso = gcnew Scripting::FileSystemObject();
Scripting::TextStream^ txtstream = fso->OpenTextFile(Application::StartupPath +
"\Products->txt",Scripting::IOMode::ForWriting, true,
Scripting::Tristate::TristateUseDefault);
for each(System::Data::DataColumn^ col in dv->Table->Columns)
{
    if (tempstr != "")
    {
        tempstr = tempstr + ";";
    }
    tempstr = tempstr + col->Caption;
}
txtstream->WriteLine(tempstr);
tempstr = "";

foreach(System::Data::DataRow^ dr in dv->Table->rows)
{
    for each(System::Data::DataColumn^ col in dv->Table->Columns)
    {
        if (tempstr != "")
        {
```

```
        tempstr = tempstr + ";";
    }
        tempstr = tempstr + "\\" + dr[col->Caption]->ToString() + "\\";
    }
    txtstream->WriteLine(tempstr);
    tempstr = "";

}
txtstream->Close();
```

SEMI-COLON DELIMITED VERTICAL VIEW

```
System::String^ tempstr = "";

Scripting::FileSystemObject^ fso = gcnew Scripting::FileSystemObject();
Scripting::TextStream^ txtstream = fso->OpenTextFile(Application::StartupPath +
"\Products->txt",Scripting::IOMode::ForWriting, true,
Scripting::Tristate::TristateUseDefault);
for each(System::Data::DataColumn^ col in dv->Table->Columns)
{
    tempstr = col->Caption;
    foreach(System::Data::DataRow^ dr in dv->Table->rows)
    {
        if (tempstr != "")
        {
            tempstr = tempstr + ";";
        }
            tempstr = tempstr + "\\" + dr[col->Caption]->ToString() + "\\";
    }
    txtstream->WriteLine(tempstr);
    tempstr = "";

}
txtstream->Close();
```

TAB DELIMITED HORIZONTAL VIEW

```
System::String^ tempstr = "";

Scripting::FileSystemObject^ fso = gcnew Scripting::FileSystemObject();
Scripting::TextStream^ txtstream = fso->OpenTextFile(Application::StartupPath +
"\Products->txt",Scripting::IOMode::ForWriting, true,
Scripting::Tristate::TristateUseDefault);
for each(System::Data::DataColumn^ col in dv->Table->Columns)
```

```
{
   if (tempstr != "")
   {
      tempstr = tempstr + "\t";
   }
   tempstr = tempstr + col->Caption;
}
txtstream->WriteLine(tempstr);
tempstr = "";

foreach(System::Data::DataRow^ dr in dv->Table->rows)
{
   for each(System::Data::DataColumn^ col in dv->Table->Columns)
   {
      if (tempstr != "")
      {
         tempstr = tempstr + "\t";
      }
      tempstr = tempstr + "\\" + dr[col->Caption]->ToString() + "\\";
   }
   txtstream->WriteLine(tempstr);
   tempstr = "";

}
txtstream->Close();
```

TAB DELIMITED VERTICAL VIEW

```
System::String^ tempstr = "";

Scripting::FileSystemObject^ fso = gcnew Scripting::FileSystemObject();
Scripting::TextStream^ txtstream = fso->OpenTextFile(Application::StartupPath +
"\Products->txt",Scripting::IOMode::ForWriting, true,
Scripting::Tristate::TristateUseDefault);
for each(System::Data::DataColumn^ col in dv->Table->Columns)
{
   tempstr = col->Caption;
   foreach(System::Data::DataRow^ dr in dv->Table->rows)
   {
      if (tempstr != "")
      {
         tempstr = tempstr + "\t";
      }
      tempstr = tempstr + "\\" + dr[col->Caption]->ToString() + "\\";
   }
   txtstream->WriteLine(tempstr);
   tempstr = "";
```

```
}
txtstream->Close();
```

TILDE DELIMITED HORIZONTAL VIEW

```
System::String^ tempstr = "";

Scripting::FileSystemObject^ fso = gcnew Scripting::FileSystemObject();
Scripting::TextStream^ txtstream = fso->OpenTextFile(Application::StartupPath +
"\Products->txt",Scripting::IOMode::ForWriting, true,
Scripting::Tristate::TristateUseDefault);
for each(System::Data::DataColumn^ col in dv->Table->Columns)
{
   if (tempstr != "")
   {
      tempstr = tempstr + "~";
   }
   tempstr = tempstr + col->Caption;
}
txtstream->WriteLine(tempstr);
tempstr = "";

foreach(System::Data::DataRow^ dr in dv->Table->rows)
{
   for each(System::Data::DataColumn^ col in dv->Table->Columns)
   {
      if (tempstr != "")
      {
         tempstr = tempstr + "~";
      }
      tempstr = tempstr + "\\" + dr[col->Caption]->ToString() + "\\";
   }
   txtstream->WriteLine(tempstr);
   tempstr = "";

}
txtstream->Close();
```

TILDE DELIMITED VERTICAL VIEW

```
System::String^ tempstr = "";

Scripting::FileSystemObject^ fso = gcnew Scripting::FileSystemObject();
```

```
Scripting::TextStream^ txtstream = fso->OpenTextFile(Application::StartupPath +
"\Products->txt",Scripting::IOMode::ForWriting, true,
Scripting::Tristate::TristateUseDefault);
for each(System::Data::DataColumn^ col in dv->Table->Columns)
{
    tempstr = col->Caption;
    foreach(System::Data::DataRow^ dr in dv->Table->rows)
    {
        if (tempstr != "")
        {
            tempstr = tempstr + "~";
        }
            tempstr = tempstr + "\\" + dr[col->Caption]->ToString() + "\\";
    }
    txtstream->WriteLine(tempstr);
    tempstr = "";

}
txtstream->Close();
```

WORKING EXCEL

The Tale of three ways you can do

it

B ELOW ARE THREE EXAMPLES ON HOW TO WORK WITH EXCEL. The first will
need a reference to Microsoft Excel.

HORIZONTAL AUTOMATION

```cpp
using namespace Microsoft::Office::Interop::Excel;

#define Excel  Microsoft::Office::Interop::Excel

Excel::Application^ oExcel = gcnew Excel::Application();
oExcel->Visible = true;
Excel::Workbook^ wb = oExcel->Workbooks->Add();
Excel::Worksheet^ ws = wb->Worksheets[1];
ws->Name = "Products";

int x = 1;
int y = 2;
```

```
int x = 1;
int y = 2;

for each(System::Data::DataColumn^ col in dv->Table->Columns)
{
   ws->Cells[1, x] = col->Caption;
   x=x+1;
}
x = 1;
   foreach(System::Data::DataRow^ dr in dv->Table->rows)
   {
     for each(System::Data::DataColumn^ col in dv->Table->Columns)
     {
     ws->Cells[y, x] = dr[col->Caption]->ToString();
     x= x + 1;
   }
   x = 1;
      y = y + 1;
   }
   ws->Columns->HorizontalAlignment = -4131;
   ws->Columns->AutoFit();
```

VERTICAL AUTOMATION

```
using namespace Microsoft::Office::Interop::Excel;

#define Excel   Microsoft::Office::Interop::Excel

   Excel::Application^ oExcel = gcnew Excel::Application();
oExcel->Visible = true;
Excel::Workbook^ wb = oExcel->Workbooks->Add();
Excel::Worksheet^ ws = wb->Worksheets[1];
ws->Name = "Products";

int x = 1;
int y = 2;

for each(System::Data::DataColumn^ col in dv->Table->Columns)
{
   ws->Cells[x, 1] = col->Caption;
   x=x+1;
}
x = 1;
   for each(System::Data::DataRow^ dr in dv->Table->rows)
   {
```

```cpp
    for each(System::Data::DataColumn^ col in dv->Table->Columns)
    {
    ws->Cells[x, y] = dr[col->Caption]->ToString();
    x= x + 1;
    }
    x = 1;
      y = y + 1;
    }
    ws->Columns->HorizontalAlignment = -4131;
    ws->Columns->AutoFit();
```

SPREADSHEET

```cpp
Scripting::FileSystemObject^ fso = gcnew Scripting::FileSystemObject();
Scripting::TextStream^ txtstream = fso->OpenTextFile(Application::StartupPath +
"\Products->xml",Scripting::IOMode::ForWriting, true,
Scripting::Tristate::TristateUseDefault);
txtstream->WriteLine("<?xml version=\"1->0\"?>");
txtstream->WriteLine("<?mso-application progid=\"Excel->Sheet\"?>");
txtstream->WriteLine("<Workbook xmlns=\"urn:schemas-microsoft-
com:office:spreadsheet\" xmlns:o=\"urn:schemas-microsoft-com:office:office\"
xmlns:x=\"urn:schemas-microsoft-com:office:excel\" xmlns:ss=\"urn:schemas-
microsoft-com:office:spreadsheet\" xmlns:html=\"http://www->w3->org/TR/REC-
html40\">");
txtstream->WriteLine("   <ExcelWorkbook xmlns=\"urn:schemas-microsoft-
com:office:excel\">");
txtstream->WriteLine("      <WindowHeight>11835</WindowHeight>");
txtstream->WriteLine("      <WindowWidth>18960</WindowWidth>");
txtstream->WriteLine("      <WindowTopX>120</WindowTopX>");
txtstream->WriteLine("      <WindowTopY>135</WindowTopY>");
txtstream->WriteLine("      <ProtectStructure>False</ProtectStructure>");
txtstream->WriteLine("      <ProtectWindows>False</ProtectWindows>");
txtstream->WriteLine("   </ExcelWorkbook>");
txtstream->WriteLine("   <Styles>");
txtstream->WriteLine("         <Style ss:ID=\"s62\">");
txtstream->WriteLine("            <Borders/>");
txtstream->WriteLine("            <Font ss:FontName=\"Calibri\"
x:Family=\"Swiss\" ss:Size=\"11\" ss:Color=\"#000000\" ss:Bold=\"1\"/>")
txtstream->WriteLine("         </Style>");
txtstream->WriteLine("         <Style ss:ID=\"s63\">");
txtstream->WriteLine("            <Alignment ss:Horizontal=\"Left\"
ss:VERTICAL=\"Bottom\" ss:Indent=\"2\"/>");
```

```
txtstream->WriteLine("                            <Font ss:FontName=\"Verdana\"
x:Family=\"Swiss\" ss:Size=\"7->7\" ss:Color=\"#000000\"/>")
txtstream->WriteLine("              </Style>");
txtstream->WriteLine(" </Styles>");
txtstream->WriteLine(" <Worksheet ss:Name=\"Win32_NetworkAdapter\">");
txtstream->WriteLine("    <Table x:FullColumns=\"1\" x:FullRows=\"1\"
ss:DefaultRowHeight=\"24->9375\">");
txtstream->WriteLine("     <Column ss:AutoFitWidth=\"1\" ss:Width=\"82->5\"
ss:Span=\"5\"/>");
txtstream->WriteLine("     <Row ss:AutoFitHeight=\"0\">");
for each(System::Data::DataColumn^ col in dv->Table->Columns)
{
    txtstream->WriteLine("       <Cell ss:StyleID=\"s62\"><Data
ss:Type=\"String\">" + col->Caption + "</Data></Cell>");
}
txtstream->WriteLine("     </Row>");
foreach(System::Data::DataRow^ dr in dv->Table->rows)
{
    txtstream->WriteLine("     <Row ss:AutoFitHeight=\"0\">");
    for each(System::Data::DataColumn^ col in dv->Table->Columns)
    {
        txtstream->WriteLine("       <Cell ss:StyleID=\"s63\"><Data
ss:Type=\"String\">" + dr[col->Caption]->ToString() + "</Data></Cell>");
    }
    txtstream->WriteLine("     </Row>");
}
txtstream->WriteLine("    </Table>");
txtstream->WriteLine(" </Worksheet>");
txtstream->WriteLine("</Workbook>");
txtstream->Close();
```

HORIZONTAL CSV

```
System::String^ tempstr = "";

Scripting::FileSystemObject^ fso = gcnew Scripting::FileSystemObject();
Scripting::TextStream^ txtstream = fso->OpenTextFile(Application::StartupPath +
"\Products->csv",Scripting::IOMode::ForWriting, true,
Scripting::Tristate::TristateUseDefault);
for each(System::Data::DataColumn^ col in dv->Table->Columns)
{
    if (tempstr != "")
    {
        tempstr = tempstr + ",";
    }
    tempstr = tempstr + col->Caption;
}
txtstream->WriteLine(tempstr);
```

```
tempstr = "";

foreach(System::Data::DataRow^ dr in dv->Table->rows)
{
   for each(System::Data::DataColumn^ col in dv->Table->Columns)
   {
      if (tempstr != "")
      {
         tempstr = tempstr + ",";
      }
      tempstr = tempstr + "\\" + dr[col->Caption]->ToString() + "\\";
   }
   txtstream->WriteLine(tempstr);
   tempstr = "";
}
txtstream->Close();

System->Diagnostics->Process->Start(Application::StartupPath +
"\\Products.csv");
```

VERTICAL CSV

```
System::String^ tempstr = "";

Scripting::FileSystemObject^ fso = gcnew Scripting::FileSystemObject();
Scripting::TextStream^ txtstream = fso->OpenTextFile(Application::StartupPath +
"\Products->csv",Scripting::IOMode::ForWriting, true,
Scripting::Tristate::TristateUseDefault);
for each(System::Data::DataColumn^ col in dv->Table->Columns)
{
   tempstr = col->Caption;
   foreach(System::Data::DataRow^ dr in dv->Table->rows)
   {
      if (tempstr != "")
      {
         tempstr = tempstr + ",";
      }
      tempstr = tempstr + "\\" + dr[col->Caption]->ToString() + "\\";
   }
   txtstream->WriteLine(tempstr);
   tempstr = "";

}
txtstream->Close();
System::Diagnostics::Process->Start(Application::StartupPath + "\\Products.csv");
```

XML Files

B ELOW ARE XML CODING EXAMPLES IN TEXT AND DOM NOTATION FOR
ATTRIBUTE XML, ELEMENT XML, ELEMENT XML FOR XSL AND SCHEMA
XML.

TEXT CREATED ATTRIBUTE XML

```
Scripting::FileSystemObject^ fso = gcnew Scripting::FileSystemObject();
Scripting::TextStream^ txtstream = fso->OpenTextFile(Application::StartupPath
+ "\\Products.xml",Scripting::IOMode::ForWriting, true,
Scripting::Tristate::TristateUseDefault);
txtstream->WriteLine("<?xml version=\"1->0\" encoding=\"iso-8859-1\"?>");
txtstream->WriteLine("<data>");
foreach(System::Data::DataRow^ dr in dv->Table->rows)
{
    txtstream->WriteLine("<products>");
    for each(System::Data::DataColumn^ col in dv->Table->Columns)
    {
        string tstr ="";
        tstr = "<property  name =\" + col->Caption + "\" ";
        tstr = tstr + " datatype = \" + col->DataType->Name + "\" ";
        tstr = tstr + " length =\" + dr[col->Caption]->ToString()->Length + "\" ";
```

```
          tstr = tstr + " value =\" + dr[col->Caption] + "\"/>";
          txtstream->WriteLine(tstr);
       }
       txtstream->WriteLine("</products>");
    }
    txtstream->WriteLine("</data>");
    txtstream->Close();
```

DOM CREATED ATTRIBUTE XML

```
XmlDocument^ xmldoc = gcnew XmlDocument();
XmlProcessingInstruction pi = xmldoc->CreateProcessingInstruction("xml",
"version='1->0' encoding='iso-8895-1'");
XmlNode^ oRoot = xmldoc->CreateElement("data");
xmldoc->AppendChild(pi);
foreach (System::Data::DataRow^ dr in dv->Table->Rows)
{
   XmlNode oNode = xmldoc->CreateNode(XmlNodeType::Element, "Products",
nullptr);
   foreach (System::Data::DataColumn^ col in dv->Table->Columns)
   {
      XmlNode^ oNode1 = xmldoc->CreateNode(XmlNodeType::Element, "Property",
nullptr);
      XmlAttribute^ oatt = xmldoc->CreateAttribute("Name");
      oatt->Value = col->Caption;
      oNode1->Attributes->SetNamedItem(oatt);
      oatt = xmldoc->CreateAttribute("datatype");
      oatt->Value = col->DataType->Name;
      oNode1->Attributes->SetNamedItem(oatt);
      oatt = xmldoc->CreateAttribute("size");
      oatt->Value = dr[col->Caption]->ToString()->Length->ToString();
      oNode1->Attributes->SetNamedItem(oatt);
      oatt = xmldoc->CreateAttribute("value");
      oatt->Value = dr[col->Caption]->ToString();
      oNode1->Attributes->SetNamedItem(oatt);
      oNode->AppendChild(oNode1);
   }
   oRoot->AppendChild(oNode);
}
xmldoc->AppendChild(oRoot);
xmldoc->Save(Application::StartupPath + "\\Products.xml");
```

TEXT CREATED ELEMENT XML

```
Scripting::FileSystemObject^ fso = gcnew Scripting::FileSystemObject();
Scripting::TextStream^ txtstream = fso->OpenTextFile(Application::StartupPath +
"\\Products.xml",Scripting::IOMode::ForWriting, true,
Scripting::Tristate::TristateUseDefault);
txtstream->WriteLine("<?xml version=\"1->0\" encoding=\"iso-8859-1\"?>");
txtstream->WriteLine("<data>");
foreach(System::Data::DataRow^ dr in dv->Table->rows)
{
   txtstream->WriteLine("<products>");
   for each(System::Data::DataColumn^ col in dv->Table->Columns)
   {
      string tstr = "";
      tstr = "<" + col->Caption + ">";
      tstr = tstr + dr[col->Caption];
      tstr = tstr + "</" + col->Caption + ">";
      txtstream->WriteLine(tstr);
   }
   txtstream->WriteLine("</products>");
}
txtstream->WriteLine("</data>");
txtstream->Close();
```

DOM CREATE ELEMENT XML

```
XmlDocument^ xmldoc = gcnew XmlDocument();
XmlProcessingInstruction^ pi = xmldoc->CreateProcessingInstruction("xml",
"version='1->0' encoding='iso-8895-1'");
XmlNode^ oRoot = xmldoc->CreateElement("data");
xmldoc->AppendChild(pi);
foreach (System::Data::DataRow^ dr in dv->Table->Rows)
{
   XmlNode^ oNode = xmldoc->CreateNode(XmlNodeType->Element, "Products",
nullptr);
   foreach (System::Data::DataColum^ col in dv->Table->Columns)
   {
```

```
    XmlNode^ oNode1 = xmldoc->CreateNode(XmlNodeType->Element, col-
>Caption, nullptr);
    oNode1->InnerText = dr[col->Caption]->ToString();
    oNode->AppendChild(oNode1);
  }
  oRoot->AppendChild(oNode);
}
xmldoc->AppendChild(oRoot);
xmldoc->Save(Application::StartupPath + "\\Products.xml");
```

TEXT CREATED ELEMENT XML FOR XLS

```
Scripting::FileSystemObject^ fso = gcnew Scripting::FileSystemObject();
Scripting::TextStream^ txtstream = fso->OpenTextFile(Application::StartupPath +
"\\Products.xml",Scripting::IOMode::ForWriting,                        true,
Scripting::Tristate::TristateUseDefault);
txtstream->WriteLine("<?xml version=\"1->0\" encoding=\"iso-8859-1\"?>");
txtstream->WriteLine("<?xml-stylesheet      type='Text/xsl'     href=\"Products-
>xsl\"?>");

txtstream->WriteLine("<data>");
foreach(System::Data::DataRow^ dr in dv->Table->rows)
{
    txtstream->WriteLine("<products>");
    for each(System::Data::DataColumn^ col in dv->Table->Columns)
    {
        string tstr = "";
        tstr = "<" + col->Caption + ">";
        tstr = tstr + dr[col->Caption]->ToString();
        tstr = tstr + "</" + col->Caption + ">";
        txtstream->WriteLine(tstr);
    }
    txtstream->WriteLine("</products>");
}
txtstream->WriteLine("</data>");
txtstream->Close();
```

DOM CREATE ELEMENT XML FOR XSL

```
XmlDocument^ xmldoc = gcnew XmlDocument();
```

```
XmlProcessingInstruction^ pi = xmldoc->CreateProcessingInstruction("xml",
"version='1->0' encoding='iso-8895-1'");
XmlProcessingInstruction^ pii = xmldoc->CreateProcessingInstruction("xml-
stylesheet", "type='text/xsl' href='Products->xsl'");
XmlNode^ oRoot = xmldoc->CreateElement("data");
xmldoc->AppendChild(pi);
xmldoc->AppendChild(pii);
foreach (System::Data::DataRow^ dr in dv->Table->Rows)
{
    XmlNode^ oNode = xmldoc->CreateNode(XmlNodeType->Element, "Products",
nullptr);
    foreach (System::Data::DataColum^ col in dv->Table->Columns)
    {
        XmlNode^ oNode1 = xmldoc->CreateNode(XmlNodeType->Element, col-
>Caption, nullptr);
        oNode1->InnerText = dr[col->Caption]->ToString();
        oNode->AppendChild(oNode1);
    }
    oRoot->AppendChild(oNode);
}
xmldoc->AppendChild(oRoot);
xmldoc->Save(Application::StartupPath + "\\Products.xml");
```

TEXT CREATED SCHEMA XML

```
Scripting::FileSystemObject^ fso = gcnew Scripting::FileSystemObject();
Scripting::TextStream^ txtstream = fso->OpenTextFile(Application::StartupPath +
"\\Products.xml",Scripting::IOMode::ForWriting,                              true,
Scripting::Tristate::TristateUseDefault);
txtstream->WriteLine("<?xml version=\"1->0\" encoding=\"iso-8859-1\"?>");
txtstream->WriteLine("<data>");
foreach(System::Data::DataRow^ dr in dv->Table->rows)
{
    txtstream->WriteLine("<products>");
    for each(System::Data::DataColumn^ col in dv->Table->Columns)
    {
```

```
       string tstr = "";
       tstr = "<" + col->Caption + ">";
       tstr = tstr + dr[col->Caption];
       tstr = tstr + "</" + col->Caption + ">";
       txtstream->WriteLine(tstr);
    }
    txtstream->WriteLine("</products>");
}
txtstream->WriteLine("</data>");
txtstream->Close();

ADODB->Recordset^ rs = gcnew ADODB->Recordset();
rs->ActiveConnection = "Provider=MSDAOSP; Data Source = MSXML2->DSOControl;
";
rs->Open(Application::StartupPath + "\\Products.xml");
rs->Save(Application::StartupPath + "\\ProductsSchema->xml");
```

DOM CREATED SCHEMA XML

```
XmlDocument^ xmldoc = new XmlDocument();
XmlProcessingInstruction^ pi = xmldoc->CreateProcessingInstruction("xml",
"version='1->0' encoding='iso-8895-1'");
XmlNode^ oRoot = xmldoc->CreateElement("data");
xmldoc->AppendChild(pi);
foreach (System::Data::DataRow^ dr in dv->Table->Rows)
{
    XmlNode^ oNode = xmldoc->CreateNode(XmlNodeType->Element, "Products",
nullptr);
    foreach (System::Data::DataColum^ col in dv->Table->Columns)
    {
        XmlNode^ oNode1 = xmldoc->CreateNode(XmlNodeType->Element, col-
>Caption, nullptr);
        oNode1->InnerText = dr[col->Caption]->ToString();
        oNode->AppendChild(oNode1);
    }
    oRoot->AppendChild(oNode);
}
xmldoc->AppendChild(oRoot);
xmldoc->Save(Application::StartupPath + "\\Products.xml");

ADODB->Recordset^ rs = gcnew ADODB->Recordset();
rs->ActiveConnection = "Provider=MSDAOSP; Data Source = MSXML2->DSOControl;
";
```

```
rs->Open(Application::StartupPath + "\\Products.xml");
rs->Save(Application::StartupPath + "\\ProductsSchema->xml");
```

XSL FILES

B ELOW ARE EXAMPLES OF WHAT YOU CAN DO WITH XSL. Views include reports and tables and orientation is for multi-line horizontal, multi-line VERTICAL, single line horizontal and single line VERTICAL.

```
Scripting::FileSystemObject^ fso = gcnew Scripting::FileSystemObject();
    Scripting::TextStream^ txtstream = fso->OpenTextFile(Application::StartupPath +
"\\Products.xsl",Scripting::IOMode::ForWriting, true,
Scripting::Tristate::TristateUseDefault);
    txtstream->WriteLine("<?xml version='1->0' encoding='UTF-8'?>");
    txtstream->WriteLine("<xsl:stylesheet version='1->0' xmlns:xsl='http://www-
>w3->org/1999/XSL/Transform'>");
    txtstream->WriteLine("<xsl:template match=\"/\">");
    txtstream->WriteLine("<html>");
    txtstream->WriteLine("<head>");
    txtstream->WriteLine("<title>Products</title>");
    txtstream->WriteLine("</head>");
    txtstream->WriteLine("<body>");
```

For Reports:

```
    txtstream->WriteLine("<table border=\"0\" colspacing=\"3\"
colpadding=\"3\">");
```

For Tables:

```
    txtstream->WriteLine("<table border=\"1\" colspacing=\"3\"
colpadding=\"3\">");
```

Single Line Horizontal

```
txtstream->WriteLine("<tr>");
for each(System::Data::DataColumn^ col in dv->Table->Columns)
{
    txtstream->WriteLine("<th align='left' nowrap='true'>" + col->Caption +
"</th>");
}
txtstream->WriteLine("</tr>");
```

None

```
txtstream->WriteLine("<tr>");
for each(System::Data::DataColumn^ col in dv->Table->Columns)
{
    txtstream->WriteLine("<td><xsl:value-of select=\"data/Products/" + col-
>Caption + "\"/></td>");
}
txtstream->WriteLine("</tr>");
```

Button

```
txtstream->WriteLine("<tr>");
for each(System::Data::DataColumn^ col in dv->Table->Columns)
{
    txtstream->WriteLine("<td  align='left' nowrap='true'><button
style='width:100%;'><xsl:value-of select=\"data/Products/" + col->Caption +
"\"/></button></td>");
}
txtstream->WriteLine("</tr>");
```

Combobox

```
txtstream->WriteLine("<tr>");
for each(System::Data::DataColumn^ col in dv->Table->Columns)
{
    txtstream->WriteLine("<td                                 align='left'
nowrap='true'><select><option><xsl:attribute           name='value'><xsl:value-of
select=\"data/Products/"  +  col->Caption  +  "\"/></xsl:attribute><xsl:value-of
select=\"data/Products/" + col->Caption  + "\"/></option></select></td>");
```

```
    }
    txtstream->WriteLine("</tr>");
```

Div

```
    txtstream->WriteLine("<tr>");
    for each(System::Data::DataColumn^ col in dv->Table->Columns)
    {
        txtstream->WriteLine("<td    align='left'  nowrap='true'><div><xsl:value-of
select=\"data/Products/" + col->Caption + "\"/></div></td>");
    }
    txtstream->WriteLine("</tr>");
```

Link

```
    txtstream->WriteLine("<tr>");
    for each(System::Data::DataColumn^ col in dv->Table->Columns)
    {
        txtstream->WriteLine("<td   align='left' nowrap='true'><a href='" + dr[col-
>Caption]->ToString() + "'><xsl:value-of select=\"data/Products/" + col->Caption
+ "\"/></a></td>");
    }
    txtstream->WriteLine("</tr>");
```

Listbox

```
    txtstream->WriteLine("<tr>");
    for each(System::Data::DataColumn^ col in dv->Table->Columns)
    {
        txtstream->WriteLine("<td              align='left'       nowrap='true'><select
multiple><option><xsl:attribute                              name='value'><xsl:value-of
select=\"data/Products/"  +  col->Caption   +   "\"/></xsl:attribute><xsl:value-of
select=\"data/Products/" + col->Caption + "\"/></option></select></td>");
    }
    txtstream->WriteLine("</tr>");
```

Span

```
    txtstream->WriteLine("<tr>");
    for each(System::Data::DataColumn^ col in dv->Table->Columns)
    {
```

```
    txtstream->WriteLine("<td    align='left'  nowrap='true'><span><xsl:value-of
select=\"data/Products/" + col->Caption + "\"/></span></td>");
    }
    txtstream->WriteLine("</tr>");
```

textarea

```
    txtstream->WriteLine("<tr>");
    for each(System::Data::DataColumn^ col in dv->Table->Columns)
    {
        txtstream->WriteLine("<td align='left' nowrap='true'><textarea><xsl:value-of
select=\"data/Products/" + col->Caption + "\"/></textarea></td>");
    }
    txtstream->WriteLine("</tr>");
```

Textbox

```
    txtstream->WriteLine("<tr>");
    for each(System::Data::DataColumn^ col in dv->Table->Columns)
    {
        txtstream->WriteLine("<td  align='left' nowrap='true'><input
type='text'><xsl:attribute name=\"value\"><xsl:value-of select=\"data/Products/" +
col->Caption + "\"/></xsl:attribute></input></td>");
    }
    txtstream->WriteLine("</tr>");
```

End code for each routine:

```
    txtstream->WriteLine("</table>");
    txtstream->WriteLine("</body>");
    txtstream->WriteLine("</html>");
    txtstream->WriteLine("</xsl:template>");
    txtstream->WriteLine("</xsl:stylesheet>");
    txtstream->Close();
```

Multi Line Horizontal

```
txtstream->WriteLine("<tr>");
for each(System::Data::DataColumn^ col in dv->Table->Columns)
{
    txtstream->WriteLine("<th align='left' nowrap='true'>" + col->Caption +
"</th>");
}
txtstream->WriteLine("</tr>");
```

None

```
txtstream->WriteLine("<xsl:for-each select=\"data/products\">");
txtstream->WriteLine("<tr>");
for each(System::Data::DataColumn^ col in dv->Table->Columns)
{
    txtstream->WriteLine("<td><xsl:value-of select=\" + col->Caption +
"\"/></td>");
}
txtstream->WriteLine("</tr>");
txtstream->WriteLine("</xsl:for-each>");
```

Button

```
txtstream->WriteLine("<xsl:for-each select=\"data/products\">");
txtstream->WriteLine("<tr>");
for each(System::Data::DataColumn^ col in dv->Table->Columns)
{
    txtstream->WriteLine("<td align='left' nowrap='true'><button
style='width:100%;'><xsl:value-of select=\" + col->Caption +
"\"/></button></td>");
}
txtstream->WriteLine("</tr>");
txtstream->WriteLine("</xsl:for-each>");
```

Combobox

```
txtstream->WriteLine("<xsl:for-each select=\"data/products\">");
txtstream->WriteLine("<tr>");
for each(System::Data::DataColumn^ col in dv->Table->Columns)
{
    txtstream->WriteLine("<td                                align='left'
nowrap='true'><select><option><xsl:attribute        name='value'><xsl:value-of
```

```
select=\\" + col->Caption  + \""/></xsl:attribute><xsl:value-of select=\\" + col-
>Caption  + "\"/></option></select></td>");
    }
    txtstream->WriteLine("</tr>");
    txtstream->WriteLine("</xsl:for-each>");
```

Div

```
    txtstream->WriteLine("<xsl:for-each select=\"data/products\">");
    txtstream->WriteLine("<tr>");
    for each(System::Data::DataColumn^ col in dv->Table->Columns)
    {
        txtstream->WriteLine("<td      align='left'  nowrap='true'><div><xsl:value-of
select=\\" + col->Caption  + "\"/></div></td>");
    }
    txtstream->WriteLine("</tr>");
    txtstream->WriteLine("</xsl:for-each>");
```

Link

```
    txtstream->WriteLine("<xsl:for-each select=\"data/products\">");
    txtstream->WriteLine("<tr>");
    for each(System::Data::DataColumn^ col in dv->Table->Columns)
    {
        txtstream->WriteLine("<td   align='left'  nowrap='true'><a href='" + dr[col-
>Caption]->ToString()  +  "'><xsl:value-of  select=\\"  +  col->Caption  +
"\"/></a></td>");
    }
    txtstream->WriteLine("</tr>");
    txtstream->WriteLine("</xsl:for-each>");
```

Listbox

```
    txtstream->WriteLine("<xsl:for-each select=\"data/products\">");
    txtstream->WriteLine("<tr>");
    for each(System::Data::DataColumn^ col in dv->Table->Columns)
    {
        txtstream->WriteLine("<td           align='left'        nowrap='true'><select
multiple><option><xsl:attribute   name='value'><xsl:value-of   select=\\"  +  col-
>Caption   +   "\"/></xsl:attribute><xsl:value-of   select=\\"  +  col->Caption   +
"\"/></option></select></td>");
    }
    txtstream->WriteLine("</tr>");
```

Span

```
txtstream->WriteLine("<xsl:for-each select=\"data/products\">");
txtstream->WriteLine("<tr>");
for each(System::Data::DataColumn^ col in dv->Table->Columns)
{
    txtstream->WriteLine("<td    align='left'  nowrap='true'><span><xsl:value-of
select=\\" + col->Caption + "\"/></span></td>");
}
txtstream->WriteLine("</tr>");
txtstream->WriteLine("</xsl:for-each>");
```

textarea

```
txtstream->WriteLine("<xsl:for-each select=\"data/products\">");
txtstream->WriteLine("<tr>");
for each(System::Data::DataColumn^ col in dv->Table->Columns)
{
    txtstream->WriteLine("<td align='left' nowrap='true'><textarea><xsl:value-of
select=\\" + col->Caption + "\"/></textarea></td>");
}
txtstream->WriteLine("</tr>");
txtstream->WriteLine("</xsl:for-each>");
```

Textbox

```
txtstream->WriteLine("<xsl:for-each select=\"data/products\">");
txtstream->WriteLine("<tr>");
for each(System::Data::DataColumn^ col in dv->Table->Columns)
{
    txtstream->WriteLine("<td align='left' nowrap='true'><input
type='text'><xsl:attribute name=\"value\"><xsl:value-of select=\\" + col->Caption
+ "\"/></xsl:attribute></input></td>");
}
txtstream->WriteLine("</tr>");
txtstream->WriteLine("</xsl:for-each>");
```

End Code for Each routine->

```
txtstream->WriteLine("</table>");
txtstream->WriteLine("</body>");
txtstream->WriteLine("</html>");
```

```
txtstream->WriteLine("</xsl:template>");
txtstream->WriteLine("</xsl:stylesheet>");
txtstream->Close();
```

Single Line VERTICAL

```
for each(System::Data::DataColumn^ col in dv->Table->Columns)
{
    txtstream->WriteLine("<tr><th align='left' nowrap='true'>" + col->Caption +
"</th>");
```

None

```
    txtstream->WriteLine("<td><xsl:value-of select=\"data/Products/" + col-
>Caption + "\"/></td></tr>");
```
Button

```
    txtstream->WriteLine("<td  align='left' nowrap='true'><button
style='width:100%;'><xsl:value-of select=\"data/Products/" + col->Caption +
"\"/></button></td></tr>");
```

Combobox

```
    txtstream->WriteLine("<td                                  align='left'
nowrap='true'><select><option><xsl:attribute          name='value'><xsl:value-of
select=\"data/Products/"   +   col->Caption   +   "\"/></xsl:attribute><xsl:value-of
select=\"data/Products/" + col->Caption + "\"/></option></select></td></tr>");
```

Div

```
    txtstream->WriteLine("<td      align='left'   nowrap='true'><div><xsl:value-of
select=\"data/Products/" + col->Caption + "\"/></div></td></tr>");
```
Link

```
    txtstream->WriteLine("<td   align='left' nowrap='true'><a href='" + dr[col-
>Caption]->ToString() + "'><xsl:value-of select=\"data/Products/" + col->Caption
+ "\"/></a></td></tr>");
```

Listbox

```
txtstream->WriteLine("<td                align='left'        nowrap='true'><select
multiple><option><xsl:attribute                        name='value'><xsl:value-of
select=\"data/Products/"    +    col->Caption     +    "\"/></xsl:attribute><xsl:value-of
select=\"data/Products/" + col->Caption  + "\"/></option></select></td></tr>");
```

Span

```
txtstream->WriteLine("<td      align='left'  nowrap='true'><span><xsl:value-of
select=\"data/Products/" + col->Caption  + "\"/></span></td></tr>");
```

textarea

```
txtstream->WriteLine("<td  align='left' nowrap='true'><textarea><xsl:value-of
select=\"data/Products/" + col->Caption  + "\"/></textarea></td></tr>");
```

Textbox

```
txtstream->WriteLine("<td  align='left' nowrap='true'><input
type='text'><xsl:attribute name=\"value\"><xsl:value-of select=\"data/Products/" +
col->Caption  + "\"/></xsl:attribute></input></td></tr>");
```

End Code for Each routine->

```
  }
  txtstream->WriteLine("</table>");
  txtstream->WriteLine("</body>");
  txtstream->WriteLine("</html>");
  txtstream->WriteLine("</xsl:template>");
  txtstream->WriteLine("</xsl:stylesheet>");
  txtstream->Close();
```

Multi Line VERTICAL

```
  for each(System::Data::DataColumn^ col in dv->Table->Columns)
  {
    txtstream->WriteLine("<tr><th align='left' nowrap='true'>" + col->Caption +
"</th>");
```

None

```
txtstream->WriteLine("<xsl:for-each select=\"data/products\">");
for each(System::Data::DataColumn^ col in dv->Table->Columns)
{
    txtstream->WriteLine("<td><xsl:value-of select=\" + col->Caption +
"\"/></td>");
}
txtstream->WriteLine("</xsl:for-each>")
txtstream->WriteLine("</tr>");
```

Button

```
txtstream->WriteLine("<xsl:for-each select=\"data/products\">");
for each(System::Data::DataColumn^ col in dv->Table->Columns)
{
    txtstream->WriteLine("<td align='left' nowrap='true'><button
style='width:100%;'><xsl:value-of select=\" + col->Caption +
"\"/></button></td>");
}
txtstream->WriteLine("</tr>");
txtstream->WriteLine("</xsl:for-each>");
```

Combobox

```
txtstream->WriteLine("<xsl:for-each select=\"data/products\">");
for each(System::Data::DataColumn^ col in dv->Table->Columns)
{
    txtstream->WriteLine("<td                              align='left'
nowrap='true'><select><option><xsl:attribute    name='value'><xsl:value-of
select=\" + col->Caption + \""/></xsl:attribute><xsl:value-of select=\" + col-
>Caption + "\"/></option></select></td>");
}
txtstream->WriteLine("</tr>");
txtstream->WriteLine("</xsl:for-each>");
```

Div

```
txtstream->WriteLine("<xsl:for-each select=\"data/products\">");
for each(System::Data::DataColumn^ col in dv->Table->Columns)
{
    txtstream->WriteLine("<td      align='left'   nowrap='true'><div><xsl:value-of
select=\" + col->Caption + "\"/></div></td>");
```

```
        }
        txtstream->WriteLine("</xsl:for-each>");
        txtstream->WriteLine("</tr>");
```

Link

```
        txtstream->WriteLine("<xsl:for-each select=\"data/products\">");
        for each(System::Data::DataColumn^ col in dv->Table->Columns)
        {
            txtstream->WriteLine("<td   align='left' nowrap='true'><a href='" + dr[col-
>Caption]->ToString()   +   "'><xsl:value-of   select=\\"   +   col->Caption   +
"\"/></a></td>");
        }
        txtstream->WriteLine("</tr>");
        txtstream->WriteLine("</xsl:for-each>");
```

Listbox

```
        txtstream->WriteLine("<xsl:for-each select=\"data/products\">");
        for each(System::Data::DataColumn^ col in dv->Table->Columns)
        {
            txtstream->WriteLine("<td            align='left'        nowrap='true'><select
multiple><option><xsl:attribute   name='value'><xsl:value-of   select=\\"   +   col-
>Caption    +   "\"/></xsl:attribute><xsl:value-of   select=\\"   +   col->Caption    +
"\"/></option></select></td>");
        }
        txtstream->WriteLine("</xsl:for-each>");
        txtstream->WriteLine("</tr>");
```

Span

```
        txtstream->WriteLine("<xsl:for-each select=\"data/products\">");
        for each(System::Data::DataColumn^ col in dv->Table->Columns)
        {
            txtstream->WriteLine("<td    align='left' nowrap='true'><span><xsl:value-of
select=\\" + col->Caption  + "\"/></span></td>");
        }
        txtstream->WriteLine("</xsl:for-each>");
        txtstream->WriteLine("</tr>");
```

textarea

```
        txtstream->WriteLine("<xsl:for-each select=\"data/products\">");
```

```
for each(System::Data::DataColumn^ col in dv->Table->Columns)
{
    txtstream->WriteLine("<td  align='left' nowrap='true'><textarea><xsl:value-of
select=\\" + col->Caption  + "\"/></textarea></td>");
}
txtstream->WriteLine("</xsl:for-each>");
txtstream->WriteLine("</tr>");
```

Textbox

```
txtstream->WriteLine("<xsl:for-each select=\"data/products\">");

for each(System::Data::DataColumn^ col in dv->Table->Columns)
{
    txtstream->WriteLine("<td  align='left' nowrap='true'><input
type='text'><xsl:attribute name=\"value\"><xsl:value-of select=\\" + col->Caption
+ "\"/></xsl:attribute></input></td>");
}
txtstream->WriteLine("</xsl:for-each>");
txtstream->WriteLine("</tr>");
```

End Code for Each routine->

```
txtstream->WriteLine("</table>");
txtstream->WriteLine("</body>");
txtstream->WriteLine("</html>");
txtstream->WriteLine("</xsl:template>");
txtstream->WriteLine("</xsl:stylesheet>");
txtstream->Close();
```

STYLESHEETS

Fuel for Thought

T HESE ARE SUPPLIED AS IS AND ARE JUST SOME IDEAS I THINK YOU WILL
LIKE. DON'T SHOOT THE MESSANGER.

None

```
txtstream->WriteLine("<style type='text/css'>");
txtstream->WriteLine("th");
txtstream->WriteLine("{");
txtstream->WriteLine("   COLOR: white;");
txtstream->WriteLine("}");
txtstream->WriteLine("td");
txtstream->WriteLine("{");
txtstream->WriteLine("   COLOR: white;");
txtstream->WriteLine("}");
txtstream->WriteLine("</style>");
```

Its A Table

```
txtstream->WriteLine("<style type='text/css'>");
txtstream->WriteLine("#itsthetable {");
txtstream->WriteLine("   font-family: Georgia, \"\"Times New Roman\"\", Times,
serif;");
txtstream->WriteLine("   color: #036;");
txtstream->WriteLine("}");
```

```
txtstream->WriteLine("caption {");
txtstream->WriteLine("    font-size: 48px;");
txtstream->WriteLine("    color: #036;");
txtstream->WriteLine("    font-weight: bolder;");
txtstream->WriteLine("    font-variant: small-caps;");
txtstream->WriteLine("}");

txtstream->WriteLine("th {");
txtstream->WriteLine("    font-size: 12px;");
txtstream->WriteLine("    color: #FFF;");
txtstream->WriteLine("    background-color: #06C;");
txtstream->WriteLine("    padding: 8px 4px;");
txtstream->WriteLine("    border-bottom: 1px solid #015ebc;");
txtstream->WriteLine("}");

txtstream->WriteLine("table {");
txtstream->WriteLine("    margin: 0;");
txtstream->WriteLine("    padding: 0;");
txtstream->WriteLine("    border-collapse: collapse;");
txtstream->WriteLine("    border: 1px solid #06C;");
txtstream->WriteLine("    width: 100%");
txtstream->WriteLine("}");

txtstream->WriteLine("#itsthetable th a:link, #itsthetable th a:visited {");
txtstream->WriteLine("    color: #FFF;");
txtstream->WriteLine("    text-decoration: none;");
txtstream->WriteLine("    border-left: 5px solid #FFF;");
txtstream->WriteLine("    padding-left: 3px;");
txtstream->WriteLine("}");

txtstream->WriteLine("th a:hover, #itsthetable th a:active {");
txtstream->WriteLine("    color: #F90;");
txtstream->WriteLine("    text-decoration: line-through;");
txtstream->WriteLine("    border-left: 5px solid #F90;");
txtstream->WriteLine("    padding-left: 3px;");
txtstream->WriteLine("}");

txtstream->WriteLine("tbody th:hover {");
txtstream->WriteLine("    background-image: url(imgs/tbody_hover->gif);");
txtstream->WriteLine("    background-position: bottom;");
txtstream->WriteLine("    background-repeat: repeat-x;");
txtstream->WriteLine("}");

txtstream->WriteLine("td {");
txtstream->WriteLine("    background-color: #f2f2f2;");
txtstream->WriteLine("    padding: 4px;");
txtstream->WriteLine("    font-size: 12px;");
txtstream->WriteLine("}");

txtstream->WriteLine("#itsthetable td:hover {");
```

```
txtstream->WriteLine("    background-color: #f8f8f8;");

txtstream->WriteLine("}");

txtstream->WriteLine("#itsthetable td a:link, #itsthetable td a:visited {");
txtstream->WriteLine("    color: #039;");
txtstream->WriteLine("    text-decoration: none;");
txtstream->WriteLine("    border-left: 3px solid #039;");
txtstream->WriteLine("    padding-left: 3px;");
txtstream->WriteLine("}");

txtstream->WriteLine("#itsthetable td a:hover, #itsthetable td a:active {");
txtstream->WriteLine("    color: #06C;");
txtstream->WriteLine("    text-decoration: line-through;");
txtstream->WriteLine("    border-left: 3px solid #06C;");
txtstream->WriteLine("    padding-left: 3px;");
txtstream->WriteLine("}");

txtstream->WriteLine("#itsthetable th {");
txtstream->WriteLine("    text-align: left;");
txtstream->WriteLine("    width: 150px;");
txtstream->WriteLine("}");

txtstream->WriteLine("#itsthetable tr {");
txtstream->WriteLine("    border-bottom: 1px solid #CCC;");
txtstream->WriteLine("}");

txtstream->WriteLine("#itsthetable thead th {");
txtstream->WriteLine("    background-image: url(imgs/thead_back->gif);");
txtstream->WriteLine("    background-repeat: repeat-x;");
txtstream->WriteLine("    background-color: #06C;");
txtstream->WriteLine("    height: 30px;");
txtstream->WriteLine("    font-size: 18px;");
txtstream->WriteLine("    text-align: center;");
txtstream->WriteLine("    text-shadow: #333 2px 2px;");
txtstream->WriteLine("    border: 2px;");
txtstream->WriteLine("}");

txtstream->WriteLine("#itsthetable tfoot th {");
txtstream->WriteLine("    background-image: url(imgs/tfoot_back->gif);");
txtstream->WriteLine("    background-repeat: repeat-x;");
txtstream->WriteLine("    background-color: #036;");
txtstream->WriteLine("    height: 30px;");
txtstream->WriteLine("    font-size: 28px;");
txtstream->WriteLine("    text-align: center;");
txtstream->WriteLine("    text-shadow: #333 2px 2px;");
txtstream->WriteLine("}");

txtstream->WriteLine("#itsthetable tfoot td {");
txtstream->WriteLine("    background-image: url(imgs/tfoot_back->gif);");
```

```
txtstream->WriteLine("    background-repeat: repeat-x;");
txtstream->WriteLine("    background-color: #036;");
txtstream->WriteLine("    color: FFF;");
txtstream->WriteLine("    height: 30px;");
txtstream->WriteLine("    font-size: 24px;");
txtstream->WriteLine("    text-align: left;");
txtstream->WriteLine("    text-shadow: #333 2px 2px;");
txtstream->WriteLine("}");

txtstream->WriteLine("tbody td a[href=\"\"http://www->csslab->cl/\"\"] {");
txtstream->WriteLine("    font-weight: bolder;");
txtstream->WriteLine("}");
txtstream->WriteLine("</style>");
```

Black and White Text

```
txtstream->WriteLine("<style type='text/css'>");
txtstream->WriteLine("th");
txtstream->WriteLine("{");
txtstream->WriteLine("    COLOR: white;");
txtstream->WriteLine("    BACKGROUND-COLOR: black;");
txtstream->WriteLine("    FONT-FAMILY: Cambria, serif;");
txtstream->WriteLine("    FONT-SIZE: 12px;");
txtstream->WriteLine("    text-align: left;");
txtstream->WriteLine("    white-Space: nowrap='nowrap';");
txtstream->WriteLine("}");
txtstream->WriteLine("td");
txtstream->WriteLine("{");
txtstream->WriteLine("    COLOR: white;");
txtstream->WriteLine("    BACKGROUND-COLOR: black;");
txtstream->WriteLine("    FONT-FAMILY: Cambria, serif;");
txtstream->WriteLine("    FONT-SIZE: 12px;");
txtstream->WriteLine("    text-align: left;");
txtstream->WriteLine("    white-Space: nowrap='nowrap';");
txtstream->WriteLine("}");
txtstream->WriteLine("div");
txtstream->WriteLine("{");
txtstream->WriteLine("    COLOR: white;");
txtstream->WriteLine("    BACKGROUND-COLOR: black;");
txtstream->WriteLine("    FONT-FAMILY: Cambria, serif;");
txtstream->WriteLine("    FONT-SIZE: 10px;");
txtstream->WriteLine("    text-align: left;");
txtstream->WriteLine("    white-Space: nowrap='nowrap';");
txtstream->WriteLine("}");
txtstream->WriteLine("span");
txtstream->WriteLine("{");
txtstream->WriteLine("    COLOR: white;");
txtstream->WriteLine("    BACKGROUND-COLOR: black;");
```

```
txtstream->WriteLine("    FONT-FAMILY: Cambria, serif;");
txtstream->WriteLine("    FONT-SIZE: 10px;");
txtstream->WriteLine("    text-align: left;");
txtstream->WriteLine("    white-Space: nowrap='nowrap';");
txtstream->WriteLine("    display:inline-block;");
txtstream->WriteLine("    width: 100%;");
txtstream->WriteLine("}");
txtstream->WriteLine("textarea");
txtstream->WriteLine("{");
txtstream->WriteLine("    COLOR: white;");
txtstream->WriteLine("    BACKGROUND-COLOR: black;");
txtstream->WriteLine("    FONT-FAMILY: Cambria, serif;");
txtstream->WriteLine("    FONT-SIZE: 10px;");
txtstream->WriteLine("    text-align: left;");
txtstream->WriteLine("    white-Space: nowrap='nowrap';");
txtstream->WriteLine("    width: 100%;");
txtstream->WriteLine("}");
txtstream->WriteLine("select");
txtstream->WriteLine("{");
txtstream->WriteLine("    COLOR: white;");
txtstream->WriteLine("    BACKGROUND-COLOR: black;");
txtstream->WriteLine("    FONT-FAMILY: Cambria, serif;");
txtstream->WriteLine("    FONT-SIZE: 10px;");
txtstream->WriteLine("    text-align: left;");
txtstream->WriteLine("    white-Space: nowrap='nowrap';");
txtstream->WriteLine("    width: 100%;");
txtstream->WriteLine("}");
txtstream->WriteLine("input");
txtstream->WriteLine("{");
txtstream->WriteLine("    COLOR: white;");
txtstream->WriteLine("    BACKGROUND-COLOR: black;");
txtstream->WriteLine("    FONT-FAMILY: Cambria, serif;");
txtstream->WriteLine("    FONT-SIZE: 12px;");
txtstream->WriteLine("    text-align: left;");
txtstream->WriteLine("    display:table-cell;");
txtstream->WriteLine("    white-Space: nowrap='nowrap';");
txtstream->WriteLine("}");
txtstream->WriteLine("h1 {");
txtstream->WriteLine("color: antiquewhite;");
txtstream->WriteLine("text-shadow: 1px 1px 1px black;");
txtstream->WriteLine("padding: 3px;");
txtstream->WriteLine("text-align: center;");
txtstream->WriteLine("box-shadow: inset 2px 2px 5px rgba(0,0,0,0->5), inset -2px
-2px 5px rgba(255,255,255,0->5);");
txtstream->WriteLine("}");
txtstream->WriteLine("</style>");
```

Colored Text

```
txtstream->WriteLine("<style type='text/css'>");
txtstream->WriteLine("th");
txtstream->WriteLine("{");
txtstream->WriteLine("    COLOR: darkred;");
txtstream->WriteLine("    BACKGROUND-COLOR: #eeeeee;");
txtstream->WriteLine("    FONT-FAMILY: Cambria, serif;");
txtstream->WriteLine("    FONT-SIZE: 12px;");
txtstream->WriteLine("    text-align: left;");
txtstream->WriteLine("    white-Space: nowrap='nowrap';");
txtstream->WriteLine("}");
txtstream->WriteLine("td");
txtstream->WriteLine("{");
txtstream->WriteLine("    COLOR: navy;");
txtstream->WriteLine("    BACKGROUND-COLOR: #eeeeee;");
txtstream->WriteLine("    FONT-FAMILY: Cambria, serif;");
txtstream->WriteLine("    FONT-SIZE: 12px;");
txtstream->WriteLine("    text-align: left;");
txtstream->WriteLine("    white-Space: nowrap='nowrap';");
txtstream->WriteLine("}");
txtstream->WriteLine("div");
txtstream->WriteLine("{");
txtstream->WriteLine("    COLOR: white;");
txtstream->WriteLine("    BACKGROUND-COLOR: navy;");
txtstream->WriteLine("    FONT-FAMILY: Cambria, serif;");
txtstream->WriteLine("    FONT-SIZE: 10px;");
txtstream->WriteLine("    text-align: left;");
txtstream->WriteLine("    white-Space: nowrap='nowrap';");
txtstream->WriteLine("}");
txtstream->WriteLine("span");
txtstream->WriteLine("{");
txtstream->WriteLine("    COLOR: white;");
txtstream->WriteLine("    BACKGROUND-COLOR: navy;");
txtstream->WriteLine("    FONT-FAMILY: Cambria, serif;");
txtstream->WriteLine("    FONT-SIZE: 10px;");
txtstream->WriteLine("    text-align: left;");
txtstream->WriteLine("    white-Space: nowrap='nowrap';");
txtstream->WriteLine("    display:inline-block;");
txtstream->WriteLine("    width: 100%;");
txtstream->WriteLine("}");
txtstream->WriteLine("textarea");
txtstream->WriteLine("{");
txtstream->WriteLine("    COLOR: white;");
txtstream->WriteLine("    BACKGROUND-COLOR: navy;");
txtstream->WriteLine("    FONT-FAMILY: Cambria, serif;");
txtstream->WriteLine("    FONT-SIZE: 10px;");
txtstream->WriteLine("    text-align: left;");
```

```
txtstream->WriteLine("    white-Space: nowrap='nowrap';");
txtstream->WriteLine("    width: 100%;");
txtstream->WriteLine("}");
txtstream->WriteLine("select");
txtstream->WriteLine("{");
txtstream->WriteLine("    COLOR: white;");
txtstream->WriteLine("    BACKGROUND-COLOR: navy;");
txtstream->WriteLine("    FONT-FAMILY:  Cambria, serif;");
txtstream->WriteLine("    FONT-SIZE: 10px;");
txtstream->WriteLine("    text-align: left;");
txtstream->WriteLine("    white-Space: nowrap='nowrap';");
txtstream->WriteLine("    width: 100%;");
txtstream->WriteLine("}");
txtstream->WriteLine("input");
txtstream->WriteLine("{");
txtstream->WriteLine("    COLOR: white;");
txtstream->WriteLine("    BACKGROUND-COLOR: navy;");
txtstream->WriteLine("    FONT-FAMILY:  Cambria, serif;");
txtstream->WriteLine("    FONT-SIZE: 12px;");
txtstream->WriteLine("    text-align: left;");
txtstream->WriteLine("    display:table-cell;");
txtstream->WriteLine("    white-Space: nowrap='nowrap';");
txtstream->WriteLine("}");
txtstream->WriteLine("h1 {");
txtstream->WriteLine("color: antiquewhite;");
txtstream->WriteLine("text-shadow: 1px 1px 1px black;");
txtstream->WriteLine("padding: 3px;");
txtstream->WriteLine("text-align: center;");
txtstream->WriteLine("box-shadow: inset 2px 2px 5px rgba(0,0,0,0->5), inset -2px
-2px 5px rgba(255,255,255,0->5);");
txtstream->WriteLine("}");
txtstream->WriteLine("</style>");
```

Oscillating Row Colors

```
txtstream->WriteLine("<style type='text/css'>");
txtstream->WriteLine("th");
txtstream->WriteLine("{");
txtstream->WriteLine("    COLOR: white;");
txtstream->WriteLine("    BACKGROUND-COLOR: navy;");
txtstream->WriteLine("    FONT-FAMILY: Cambria, serif;");
txtstream->WriteLine("    FONT-SIZE: 12px;");
txtstream->WriteLine("    text-align: left;");
txtstream->WriteLine("    white-Space: nowrap='nowrap';");
txtstream->WriteLine("}");
txtstream->WriteLine("td");
txtstream->WriteLine("{");
```

```
txtstream->WriteLine("    COLOR: navy;");
txtstream->WriteLine("    FONT-FAMILY: Cambria, serif;");
txtstream->WriteLine("    FONT-SIZE: 12px;");
txtstream->WriteLine("    text-align: left;");
txtstream->WriteLine("    white-Space: nowrap='nowrap';");
txtstream->WriteLine("}");
txtstream->WriteLine("div");
txtstream->WriteLine("{");
txtstream->WriteLine("    COLOR: navy;");
txtstream->WriteLine("    FONT-FAMILY: Cambria, serif;");
txtstream->WriteLine("    FONT-SIZE: 12px;");
txtstream->WriteLine("    text-align: left;");
txtstream->WriteLine("    white-Space: nowrap='nowrap';");
txtstream->WriteLine("}");
txtstream->WriteLine("span");
txtstream->WriteLine("{");
txtstream->WriteLine("    COLOR: navy;");
txtstream->WriteLine("    FONT-FAMILY: Cambria, serif;");
txtstream->WriteLine("    FONT-SIZE: 12px;");
txtstream->WriteLine("    text-align: left;");
txtstream->WriteLine("    white-Space: nowrap='nowrap';");
txtstream->WriteLine("    width: 100%;");
txtstream->WriteLine("}");
txtstream->WriteLine("textarea");
txtstream->WriteLine("{");
txtstream->WriteLine("    COLOR: navy;");
txtstream->WriteLine("    FONT-FAMILY: Cambria, serif;");
txtstream->WriteLine("    FONT-SIZE: 12px;");
txtstream->WriteLine("    text-align: left;");
txtstream->WriteLine("    white-Space: nowrap='nowrap';");
txtstream->WriteLine("    display:inline-block;");
txtstream->WriteLine("    width: 100%;");
txtstream->WriteLine("}");
txtstream->WriteLine("select");
txtstream->WriteLine("{");
txtstream->WriteLine("    COLOR: navy;");
txtstream->WriteLine("    FONT-FAMILY: Cambria, serif;");
txtstream->WriteLine("    FONT-SIZE: 10px;");
txtstream->WriteLine("    text-align: left;");
txtstream->WriteLine("    white-Space: nowrap='nowrap';");
txtstream->WriteLine("    display:inline-block;");
txtstream->WriteLine("    width: 100%;");
txtstream->WriteLine("}");
txtstream->WriteLine("input");
txtstream->WriteLine("{");
txtstream->WriteLine("    COLOR: navy;");
txtstream->WriteLine("    FONT-FAMILY: Cambria, serif;");
txtstream->WriteLine("    FONT-SIZE: 12px;");
txtstream->WriteLine("    text-align: left;");
txtstream->WriteLine("    display:table-cell;");
```

```
txtstream->WriteLine("    white-Space: nowrap='nowrap';");
txtstream->WriteLine("}");
txtstream->WriteLine("h1 {");
txtstream->WriteLine("color: antiquewhite;");
txtstream->WriteLine("text-shadow: 1px 1px 1px black;");
txtstream->WriteLine("padding: 3px;");
txtstream->WriteLine("text-align: center;");
txtstream->WriteLine("box-shadow: inset 2px 2px 5px rgba(0,0,0,0->5), inset -2px -2px 5px rgba(255,255,255,0->5);");
txtstream->WriteLine("}");
txtstream->WriteLine("tr:nth-child(even){background-color:#f2f2f2;}");
txtstream->WriteLine("tr:nth-child(odd){background-color:#cccccc; color:#f2f2f2;}");
txtstream->WriteLine("</style>");
```

Ghost Decorated

```
txtstream->WriteLine("<style type='text/css'>");
txtstream->WriteLine("th");
txtstream->WriteLine("{");
txtstream->WriteLine("    COLOR: black;");
txtstream->WriteLine("    BACKGROUND-COLOR: white;");
txtstream->WriteLine("    FONT-FAMILY: Cambria, serif;");
txtstream->WriteLine("    FONT-SIZE: 12px;");
txtstream->WriteLine("    text-align: left;");
txtstream->WriteLine("    white-Space: nowrap='nowrap';");
txtstream->WriteLine("}");
txtstream->WriteLine("td");
txtstream->WriteLine("{");
txtstream->WriteLine("    COLOR: black;");
txtstream->WriteLine("    BACKGROUND-COLOR: white;");
txtstream->WriteLine("    FONT-FAMILY: Cambria, serif;");
txtstream->WriteLine("    FONT-SIZE: 12px;");
txtstream->WriteLine("    text-align: left;");
txtstream->WriteLine("    white-Space: nowrap='nowrap';");
txtstream->WriteLine("}");
txtstream->WriteLine("div");
txtstream->WriteLine("{");
txtstream->WriteLine("    COLOR: black;");
txtstream->WriteLine("    BACKGROUND-COLOR: white;");
txtstream->WriteLine("    FONT-FAMILY: Cambria, serif;");
txtstream->WriteLine("    FONT-SIZE: 10px;");
txtstream->WriteLine("    text-align: left;");
txtstream->WriteLine("    white-Space: nowrap='nowrap';");
txtstream->WriteLine("}");
txtstream->WriteLine("span");
txtstream->WriteLine("{");
txtstream->WriteLine("    COLOR: black;");
txtstream->WriteLine("    BACKGROUND-COLOR: white;");
```

```
txtstream->WriteLine("    FONT-FAMILY:  Cambria, serif;");
txtstream->WriteLine("    FONT-SIZE: 10px;");
txtstream->WriteLine("    text-align: left;");
txtstream->WriteLine("    white-Space: nowrap='nowrap';");
txtstream->WriteLine("    display:inline-block;");
txtstream->WriteLine("    width: 100%;");
txtstream->WriteLine("}");
txtstream->WriteLine("textarea");
txtstream->WriteLine("{");
txtstream->WriteLine("    COLOR: black;");
txtstream->WriteLine("    BACKGROUND-COLOR: white;");
txtstream->WriteLine("    FONT-FAMILY:  Cambria, serif;");
txtstream->WriteLine("    FONT-SIZE: 10px;");
txtstream->WriteLine("    text-align: left;");
txtstream->WriteLine("    white-Space: nowrap='nowrap';");
txtstream->WriteLine("    width: 100%;");
txtstream->WriteLine("}");
txtstream->WriteLine("select");
txtstream->WriteLine("{");
txtstream->WriteLine("    COLOR: black;");
txtstream->WriteLine("    BACKGROUND-COLOR: white;");
txtstream->WriteLine("    FONT-FAMILY:  Cambria, serif;");
txtstream->WriteLine("    FONT-SIZE: 10px;");
txtstream->WriteLine("    text-align: left;");
txtstream->WriteLine("    white-Space: nowrap='nowrap';");
txtstream->WriteLine("    width: 100%;");
txtstream->WriteLine("}");
txtstream->WriteLine("input");
txtstream->WriteLine("{");
txtstream->WriteLine("    COLOR: black;");
txtstream->WriteLine("    BACKGROUND-COLOR: white;");
txtstream->WriteLine("    FONT-FAMILY:  Cambria, serif;");
txtstream->WriteLine("    FONT-SIZE: 12px;");
txtstream->WriteLine("    text-align: left;");
txtstream->WriteLine("    display:table-cell;");
txtstream->WriteLine("    white-Space: nowrap='nowrap';");
txtstream->WriteLine("}");
txtstream->WriteLine("h1 {");
txtstream->WriteLine("color: antiquewhite;");
txtstream->WriteLine("text-shadow: 1px 1px 1px black;");
txtstream->WriteLine("padding: 3px;");
txtstream->WriteLine("text-align: center;");
txtstream->WriteLine("box-shadow: inset 2px 2px 5px rgba(0,0,0,0->5), inset -2px
-2px 5px rgba(255,255,255,0->5);");
txtstream->WriteLine("}");
txtstream->WriteLine("</style>");
```

```
txtstream->WriteLine("<style type='text/css'>");
txtstream->WriteLine("body");
txtstream->WriteLine("{");
txtstream->WriteLine("    PADDING-RIGHT: 0px;");
txtstream->WriteLine("    PADDING-LEFT: 0px;");
txtstream->WriteLine("    PADDING-BOTTOM: 0px;");
txtstream->WriteLine("    MARGIN: 0px;");
txtstream->WriteLine("    COLOR: #333;");
txtstream->WriteLine("    PADDING-TOP: 0px;");
txtstream->WriteLine("    FONT-FAMILY: verdana, arial, helvetica, sans-serif;");
txtstream->WriteLine("}");
txtstream->WriteLine("table");
txtstream->WriteLine("{");
txtstream->WriteLine("    BORDER-RIGHT: #999999 3px solid;");
txtstream->WriteLine("    PADDING-RIGHT: 6px;");
txtstream->WriteLine("    PADDING-LEFT: 6px;");
txtstream->WriteLine("    FONT-WEIGHT: Bold;");
txtstream->WriteLine("    FONT-SIZE: 14px;");
txtstream->WriteLine("    PADDING-BOTTOM: 6px;");
txtstream->WriteLine("    COLOR: Peru;");
txtstream->WriteLine("    LINE-HEIGHT: 14px;");
txtstream->WriteLine("    PADDING-TOP: 6px;");
txtstream->WriteLine("    BORDER-BOTTOM: #999 1px solid;");
txtstream->WriteLine("    BACKGROUND-COLOR: #eeeeee;");
txtstream->WriteLine("    FONT-FAMILY: verdana, arial, helvetica, sans-serif;");
txtstream->WriteLine("    FONT-SIZE: 12px;");
txtstream->WriteLine("}");
txtstream->WriteLine("th");
txtstream->WriteLine("{");
txtstream->WriteLine("    BORDER-RIGHT: #999999 3px solid;");
txtstream->WriteLine("    PADDING-RIGHT: 6px;");
txtstream->WriteLine("    PADDING-LEFT: 6px;");
txtstream->WriteLine("    FONT-WEIGHT: Bold;");
txtstream->WriteLine("    FONT-SIZE: 14px;");
txtstream->WriteLine("    PADDING-BOTTOM: 6px;");
txtstream->WriteLine("    COLOR: darkred;");
txtstream->WriteLine("    LINE-HEIGHT: 14px;");
txtstream->WriteLine("    PADDING-TOP: 6px;");
txtstream->WriteLine("    BORDER-BOTTOM: #999 1px solid;");
txtstream->WriteLine("    BACKGROUND-COLOR: #eeeeee;");
txtstream->WriteLine("    FONT-FAMILY: Cambria, serif;");
txtstream->WriteLine("    FONT-SIZE: 12px;");
txtstream->WriteLine("    text-align: left;");
txtstream->WriteLine("    white-Space: nowrap='nowrap';");
txtstream->WriteLine("}");
```

```
txtstream->WriteLine("->th");
txtstream->WriteLine("{");
txtstream->WriteLine("    BORDER-RIGHT: #999999 2px solid;");
txtstream->WriteLine("    PADDING-RIGHT: 6px;");
txtstream->WriteLine("    PADDING-LEFT: 6px;");
txtstream->WriteLine("    FONT-WEIGHT: Bold;");
txtstream->WriteLine("    PADDING-BOTTOM: 6px;");
txtstream->WriteLine("    COLOR: black;");
txtstream->WriteLine("    PADDING-TOP: 6px;");
txtstream->WriteLine("    BORDER-BOTTOM: #999 2px solid;");
txtstream->WriteLine("    BACKGROUND-COLOR: #eeeeee;");
txtstream->WriteLine("    FONT-FAMILY:  Cambria, serif;");
txtstream->WriteLine("    FONT-SIZE: 10px;");
txtstream->WriteLine("    text-align: right;");
txtstream->WriteLine("    white-Space: nowrap='nowrap';");
txtstream->WriteLine("}");
txtstream->WriteLine("td");
txtstream->WriteLine("{");
txtstream->WriteLine("    BORDER-RIGHT: #999999 3px solid;");
txtstream->WriteLine("    PADDING-RIGHT: 6px;");
txtstream->WriteLine("    PADDING-LEFT: 6px;");
txtstream->WriteLine("    FONT-WEIGHT: Normal;");
txtstream->WriteLine("    PADDING-BOTTOM: 6px;");
txtstream->WriteLine("    COLOR: navy;");
txtstream->WriteLine("    LINE-HEIGHT: 14px;");
txtstream->WriteLine("    PADDING-TOP: 6px;");
txtstream->WriteLine("    BORDER-BOTTOM: #999 1px solid;");
txtstream->WriteLine("    BACKGROUND-COLOR: #eeeeee;");
txtstream->WriteLine("    FONT-FAMILY:  Cambria, serif;");
txtstream->WriteLine("    FONT-SIZE: 12px;");
txtstream->WriteLine("    text-align: left;");
txtstream->WriteLine("    white-Space: nowrap='nowrap';");
txtstream->WriteLine("}");
txtstream->WriteLine("div");
txtstream->WriteLine("{");
txtstream->WriteLine("    BORDER-RIGHT: #999999 3px solid;");
txtstream->WriteLine("    PADDING-RIGHT: 6px;");
txtstream->WriteLine("    PADDING-LEFT: 6px;");
txtstream->WriteLine("    FONT-WEIGHT: Normal;");
txtstream->WriteLine("    PADDING-BOTTOM: 6px;");
txtstream->WriteLine("    COLOR: white;");
txtstream->WriteLine("    PADDING-TOP: 6px;");
txtstream->WriteLine("    BORDER-BOTTOM: #999 1px solid;");
txtstream->WriteLine("    BACKGROUND-COLOR: navy;");
txtstream->WriteLine("    FONT-FAMILY:  Cambria, serif;");
txtstream->WriteLine("    FONT-SIZE: 10px;");
txtstream->WriteLine("    text-align: left;");
txtstream->WriteLine("    white-Space: nowrap='nowrap';");
txtstream->WriteLine("}");
txtstream->WriteLine("span");
```

```
txtstream->WriteLine("{");
txtstream->WriteLine("    BORDER-RIGHT: #999999 3px solid;");
txtstream->WriteLine("    PADDING-RIGHT: 3px;");
txtstream->WriteLine("    PADDING-LEFT: 3px;");
txtstream->WriteLine("    FONT-WEIGHT: Normal;");
txtstream->WriteLine("    PADDING-BOTTOM: 3px;");
txtstream->WriteLine("    COLOR: white;");
txtstream->WriteLine("    PADDING-TOP: 3px;");
txtstream->WriteLine("    BORDER-BOTTOM: #999 1px solid;");
txtstream->WriteLine("    BACKGROUND-COLOR: navy;");
txtstream->WriteLine("    FONT-FAMILY: Cambria, serif;");
txtstream->WriteLine("    FONT-SIZE: 10px;");
txtstream->WriteLine("    text-align: left;");
txtstream->WriteLine("    white-Space: nowrap='nowrap';");
txtstream->WriteLine("    display:inline-block;");
txtstream->WriteLine("    width: 100%;");
txtstream->WriteLine("}");
txtstream->WriteLine("textarea");
txtstream->WriteLine("{");
txtstream->WriteLine("    BORDER-RIGHT: #999999 3px solid;");
txtstream->WriteLine("    PADDING-RIGHT: 3px;");
txtstream->WriteLine("    PADDING-LEFT: 3px;");
txtstream->WriteLine("    FONT-WEIGHT: Normal;");
txtstream->WriteLine("    PADDING-BOTTOM: 3px;");
txtstream->WriteLine("    COLOR: white;");
txtstream->WriteLine("    PADDING-TOP: 3px;");
txtstream->WriteLine("    BORDER-BOTTOM: #999 1px solid;");
txtstream->WriteLine("    BACKGROUND-COLOR: navy;");
txtstream->WriteLine("    FONT-FAMILY: Cambria, serif;");
txtstream->WriteLine("    FONT-SIZE: 10px;");
txtstream->WriteLine("    text-align: left;");
txtstream->WriteLine("    white-Space: nowrap='nowrap';");
txtstream->WriteLine("    width: 100%;");
txtstream->WriteLine("}");
txtstream->WriteLine("select");
txtstream->WriteLine("{");
txtstream->WriteLine("    BORDER-RIGHT: #999999 3px solid;");
txtstream->WriteLine("    PADDING-RIGHT: 6px;");
txtstream->WriteLine("    PADDING-LEFT: 6px;");
txtstream->WriteLine("    FONT-WEIGHT: Normal;");
txtstream->WriteLine("    PADDING-BOTTOM: 6px;");
txtstream->WriteLine("    COLOR: white;");
txtstream->WriteLine("    PADDING-TOP: 6px;");
txtstream->WriteLine("    BORDER-BOTTOM: #999 1px solid;");
txtstream->WriteLine("    BACKGROUND-COLOR: navy;");
txtstream->WriteLine("    FONT-FAMILY: Cambria, serif;");
txtstream->WriteLine("    FONT-SIZE: 10px;");
txtstream->WriteLine("    text-align: left;");
txtstream->WriteLine("    white-Space: nowrap='nowrap';");
txtstream->WriteLine("    width: 100%;");
```

```
txtstream->WriteLine("}");
txtstream->WriteLine("input");
txtstream->WriteLine("{");
txtstream->WriteLine("    BORDER-RIGHT: #999999 3px solid;");
txtstream->WriteLine("    PADDING-RIGHT: 3px;");
txtstream->WriteLine("    PADDING-LEFT: 3px;");
txtstream->WriteLine("    FONT-WEIGHT: Bold;");
txtstream->WriteLine("    PADDING-BOTTOM: 3px;");
txtstream->WriteLine("    COLOR: white;");
txtstream->WriteLine("    PADDING-TOP: 3px;");
txtstream->WriteLine("    BORDER-BOTTOM: #999 1px solid;");
txtstream->WriteLine("    BACKGROUND-COLOR: navy;");
txtstream->WriteLine("    FONT-FAMILY: Cambria, serif;");
txtstream->WriteLine("    FONT-SIZE: 12px;");
txtstream->WriteLine("    text-align: left;");
txtstream->WriteLine("    display:table-cell;");
txtstream->WriteLine("    white-Space: nowrap='nowrap';");
txtstream->WriteLine("    width: 100%;");
txtstream->WriteLine("}");
txtstream->WriteLine("h1 {");
txtstream->WriteLine("color: antiquewhite;");
txtstream->WriteLine("text-shadow: 1px 1px 1px black;");
txtstream->WriteLine("padding: 3px;");
txtstream->WriteLine("text-align: center;");
txtstream->WriteLine("box-shadow: inset 2px 2px 5px rgba(0,0,0,0->5), inset -2px -2px 5px rgba(255,255,255,0->5);");
txtstream->WriteLine("}");
txtstream->WriteLine("</style>");
```

Shadow Box

```
txtstream->WriteLine("<style type='text/css'>");
txtstream->WriteLine("body");
txtstream->WriteLine("{");
txtstream->WriteLine("    PADDING-RIGHT: 0px;");
txtstream->WriteLine("    PADDING-LEFT: 0px;");
txtstream->WriteLine("    PADDING-BOTTOM: 0px;");
txtstream->WriteLine("    MARGIN: 0px;");
txtstream->WriteLine("    COLOR: #333;");
txtstream->WriteLine("    PADDING-TOP: 0px;");
txtstream->WriteLine("    FONT-FAMILY: verdana, arial, helvetica, sans-serif;");
txtstream->WriteLine("}");
txtstream->WriteLine("table");
txtstream->WriteLine("{");
txtstream->WriteLine("    BORDER-RIGHT: #999999 1px solid;");
txtstream->WriteLine("    PADDING-RIGHT: 1px;");
txtstream->WriteLine("    PADDING-LEFT: 1px;");
txtstream->WriteLine("    PADDING-BOTTOM: 1px;");
txtstream->WriteLine("    LINE-HEIGHT: 8px;");
```

```
txtstream->WriteLine("    PADDING-TOP: 1px;");
txtstream->WriteLine("    BORDER-BOTTOM: #999 1px solid;");
txtstream->WriteLine("    BACKGROUND-COLOR: #eeeeee;");
txtstream->WriteLine("    filter:progid:DXImageTransform->Microsoft->Shadow(color='silver', Direction=135, Strength=16)");
txtstream->WriteLine("}");
txtstream->WriteLine("th");
txtstream->WriteLine("{");
txtstream->WriteLine("    BORDER-RIGHT: #999999 3px solid;");
txtstream->WriteLine("    PADDING-RIGHT: 6px;");
txtstream->WriteLine("    PADDING-LEFT: 6px;");
txtstream->WriteLine("    FONT-WEIGHT: Bold;");
txtstream->WriteLine("    FONT-SIZE: 14px;");
txtstream->WriteLine("    PADDING-BOTTOM: 6px;");
txtstream->WriteLine("    COLOR: darkred;");
txtstream->WriteLine("    LINE-HEIGHT: 14px;");
txtstream->WriteLine("    PADDING-TOP: 6px;");
txtstream->WriteLine("    BORDER-BOTTOM: #999 1px solid;");
txtstream->WriteLine("    BACKGROUND-COLOR: #eeeeee;");
txtstream->WriteLine("    FONT-FAMILY: Cambria, serif;");
txtstream->WriteLine("    FONT-SIZE: 12px;");
txtstream->WriteLine("    text-align: left;");
txtstream->WriteLine("    white-Space: nowrap='nowrap';");
txtstream->WriteLine("}");
txtstream->WriteLine("->th");
txtstream->WriteLine("{");
txtstream->WriteLine("    BORDER-RIGHT: #999999 2px solid;");
txtstream->WriteLine("    PADDING-RIGHT: 6px;");
txtstream->WriteLine("    PADDING-LEFT: 6px;");
txtstream->WriteLine("    FONT-WEIGHT: Bold;");
txtstream->WriteLine("    PADDING-BOTTOM: 6px;");
txtstream->WriteLine("    COLOR: black;");
txtstream->WriteLine("    PADDING-TOP: 6px;");
txtstream->WriteLine("    BORDER-BOTTOM: #999 2px solid;");
txtstream->WriteLine("    BACKGROUND-COLOR: #eeeeee;");
txtstream->WriteLine("    FONT-FAMILY: Cambria, serif;");
txtstream->WriteLine("    FONT-SIZE: 10px;");
txtstream->WriteLine("    text-align: right;");
txtstream->WriteLine("    white-Space: nowrap='nowrap';");
txtstream->WriteLine("}");
txtstream->WriteLine("td");
txtstream->WriteLine("{");
txtstream->WriteLine("    BORDER-RIGHT: #999999 3px solid;");
txtstream->WriteLine("    PADDING-RIGHT: 6px;");
txtstream->WriteLine("    PADDING-LEFT: 6px;");
txtstream->WriteLine("    FONT-WEIGHT: Normal;");
txtstream->WriteLine("    PADDING-BOTTOM: 6px;");
txtstream->WriteLine("    COLOR: navy;");
txtstream->WriteLine("    LINE-HEIGHT: 14px;");
txtstream->WriteLine("    PADDING-TOP: 6px;");
```

```
txtstream->WriteLine("    BORDER-BOTTOM: #999 1px solid;");
txtstream->WriteLine("    BACKGROUND-COLOR: #eeeeee;");
txtstream->WriteLine("    FONT-FAMILY: Cambria, serif;");
txtstream->WriteLine("    FONT-SIZE: 12px;");
txtstream->WriteLine("    text-align: left;");
txtstream->WriteLine("    white-Space: nowrap='nowrap';");
txtstream->WriteLine("}");
txtstream->WriteLine("div");
txtstream->WriteLine("{");
txtstream->WriteLine("    BORDER-RIGHT: #999999 3px solid;");
txtstream->WriteLine("    PADDING-RIGHT: 6px;");
txtstream->WriteLine("    PADDING-LEFT: 6px;");
txtstream->WriteLine("    FONT-WEIGHT: Normal;");
txtstream->WriteLine("    PADDING-BOTTOM: 6px;");
txtstream->WriteLine("    COLOR: white;");
txtstream->WriteLine("    PADDING-TOP: 6px;");
txtstream->WriteLine("    BORDER-BOTTOM: #999 1px solid;");
txtstream->WriteLine("    BACKGROUND-COLOR: navy;");
txtstream->WriteLine("    FONT-FAMILY: Cambria, serif;");
txtstream->WriteLine("    FONT-SIZE: 10px;");
txtstream->WriteLine("    text-align: left;");
txtstream->WriteLine("    white-Space: nowrap='nowrap';");
txtstream->WriteLine("}");
txtstream->WriteLine("span");
txtstream->WriteLine("{");
txtstream->WriteLine("    BORDER-RIGHT: #999999 3px solid;");
txtstream->WriteLine("    PADDING-RIGHT: 3px;");
txtstream->WriteLine("    PADDING-LEFT: 3px;");
txtstream->WriteLine("    FONT-WEIGHT: Normal;");
txtstream->WriteLine("    PADDING-BOTTOM: 3px;");
txtstream->WriteLine("    COLOR: white;");
txtstream->WriteLine("    PADDING-TOP: 3px;");
txtstream->WriteLine("    BORDER-BOTTOM: #999 1px solid;");
txtstream->WriteLine("    BACKGROUND-COLOR: navy;");
txtstream->WriteLine("    FONT-FAMILY: Cambria, serif;");
txtstream->WriteLine("    FONT-SIZE: 10px;");
txtstream->WriteLine("    text-align: left;");
txtstream->WriteLine("    white-Space: nowrap='nowrap';");
txtstream->WriteLine("    display: inline-block;");
txtstream->WriteLine("    width: 100%;");
txtstream->WriteLine("}");
txtstream->WriteLine("textarea");
txtstream->WriteLine("{");
txtstream->WriteLine("    BORDER-RIGHT: #999999 3px solid;");
txtstream->WriteLine("    PADDING-RIGHT: 3px;");
txtstream->WriteLine("    PADDING-LEFT: 3px;");
txtstream->WriteLine("    FONT-WEIGHT: Normal;");
txtstream->WriteLine("    PADDING-BOTTOM: 3px;");
txtstream->WriteLine("    COLOR: white;");
txtstream->WriteLine("    PADDING-TOP: 3px;");
```

```
txtstream->WriteLine("    BORDER-BOTTOM: #999 1px solid;");
txtstream->WriteLine("    BACKGROUND-COLOR: navy;");
txtstream->WriteLine("    FONT-FAMILY: Cambria, serif;");
txtstream->WriteLine("    FONT-SIZE: 10px;");
txtstream->WriteLine("    text-align: left;");
txtstream->WriteLine("    white-Space: nowrap='nowrap';");
txtstream->WriteLine("    width: 100%;");
txtstream->WriteLine("}");
txtstream->WriteLine("select");
txtstream->WriteLine("{");
txtstream->WriteLine("    BORDER-RIGHT: #999999 3px solid;");
txtstream->WriteLine("    PADDING-RIGHT: 6px;");
txtstream->WriteLine("    PADDING-LEFT: 6px;");
txtstream->WriteLine("    FONT-WEIGHT: Normal;");
txtstream->WriteLine("    PADDING-BOTTOM: 6px;");
txtstream->WriteLine("    COLOR: white;");
txtstream->WriteLine("    PADDING-TOP: 6px;");
txtstream->WriteLine("    BORDER-BOTTOM: #999 1px solid;");
txtstream->WriteLine("    BACKGROUND-COLOR: navy;");
txtstream->WriteLine("    FONT-FAMILY: Cambria, serif;");
txtstream->WriteLine("    FONT-SIZE: 10px;");
txtstream->WriteLine("    text-align: left;");
txtstream->WriteLine("    white-Space: nowrap='nowrap';");
txtstream->WriteLine("    width: 100%;");
txtstream->WriteLine("}");
txtstream->WriteLine("input");
txtstream->WriteLine("{");
txtstream->WriteLine("    BORDER-RIGHT: #999999 3px solid;");
txtstream->WriteLine("    PADDING-RIGHT: 3px;");
txtstream->WriteLine("    PADDING-LEFT: 3px;");
txtstream->WriteLine("    FONT-WEIGHT: Bold;");
txtstream->WriteLine("    PADDING-BOTTOM: 3px;");
txtstream->WriteLine("    COLOR: white;");
txtstream->WriteLine("    PADDING-TOP: 3px;");
txtstream->WriteLine("    BORDER-BOTTOM: #999 1px solid;");
txtstream->WriteLine("    BACKGROUND-COLOR: navy;");
txtstream->WriteLine("    FONT-FAMILY: Cambria, serif;");
txtstream->WriteLine("    FONT-SIZE: 12px;");
txtstream->WriteLine("    text-align: left;");
txtstream->WriteLine("    display: table-cell;");
txtstream->WriteLine("    white-Space: nowrap='nowrap';");
txtstream->WriteLine("    width: 100%;");
txtstream->WriteLine("}");
txtstream->WriteLine("h1 {");
txtstream->WriteLine("color: antiquewhite;");
txtstream->WriteLine("text-shadow: 1px 1px 1px black;");
txtstream->WriteLine("padding: 3px;");
txtstream->WriteLine("text-align: center;");
txtstream->WriteLine("box-shadow: inset 2px 2px 5px rgba(0,0,0,0->5), inset -2px
-2px 5px rgba(255,255,255,0->5);");
```

```
txtstream->WriteLine("}");
txtstream->WriteLine("</style>");
```

www.ingramcontent.com/pod-product-compliance
Lightning Source LLC
Chambersburg PA
CBHW070850070326
40690CB00009B/1772